Hodder Primary PE

DANCE

Maureen Douglas

Hodder & Stoughton

A MEMBER OF THE HODDER HEADLINE GROUP

Acknowledgements

The poem 'A Lazy Thought' on page 49 © 1962 Eve Merriam. The poems 'Snow Play', page 48 and 'The Wrigglebug Dance', page 49, are by the author, Maureen Douglas.

Orders: please contact Bookpoint Ltd, 39 Milton Park, Abingdon, Oxon OX14 4TD. Telephone: (44) 01235 400414, Fax: (44) 01235 400454. Lines are open from 9.00–6.00, Monday to Saturday, with a 24 hour message answering service. Email address: orders@bookpoint.co.uk

British Library Cataloguing in Publication Data
A catalogue record for this title is available from The British Library

ISBN 0 340 67374 5

First published 1999
Impression number   10 9 8 7 6 5 4 3 2 1
Year   2005 2004 2003 2002 2001 2000 1999

Typeset by Fakenham Photosetting Ltd, Fakenham, Norfolk.
Printed in Great Britain for Hodder & Stoughton Educational, a division of Hodder Headline Plc, 338 Euston Road, London NW1 3BH by Redwood Books, Trowbridge, Wiltshire.

Contents

Preface

This book is written for teachers and those training to teach in the primary school. The intention is to make dance accessible to teachers and through them to children. It is designed to give confidence to the teacher promoting understanding of movement, dance making, and the content and process of teaching dance.

Like many other dance books this one has ideas for lessons but it also addresses the elements of good practice implicit in the requirements of the 1995 National Curriculum for Physical Education. The planning, teaching, and assessment of the subject are all discussed. The material in the book will support the development of dance throughout the primary school. Review will lead to a new Physical Education Curriculum for the year 2000. It may be articulated and presented differently, but it will embody good practice and the processes of dance will remain constant. This text will be relevant to a new curriculum statement.

This is a practical text underpinned by theory. The dance work described in each chapter has been undertaken in schools, and the processes of identifying lesson content and planning have been used by students and teachers.

Dance is for doing and for enjoying. It is to be hoped that this book will encourage teachers to begin and develop their dance work and that the children's enthusiasm will inspire them to develop dance in the school.

Acknowledgements

Acknowledgements to all the children, students and teachers with whom I have worked and from whom I continue to learn. Particular thanks to the children and staff of Brixington Infant's School, Brixington Junior School and St Joseph's Primary School Exmouth and Stoke Hill First School Exeter who feature in the photographs, to Alan Gentle for the photography, Alison Holdstock for computer assistance and to colleagues and friends for all their support and encouragement.

Why dance? A rationale for dance and dance teaching

Dance is one of the areas of activity included in the National Curriculum for Physical Education at both Key Stages 1 and 2. Effective delivery of the curriculum requires understanding of what we teach and this chapter examines the place of dance within the National Curriculum, its nature as an art form and the contribution it can make to the education of children.

DANCE WITHIN PHYSICAL EDUCATION

As a part of the Physical Education curriculum dance contributes to the child's total development. Through a carefully structured PE programme the child can gain understanding of the medium of movement as well as awareness and control of the moving body. The discipline of physical education is concerned with the development of the movement ability and of the whole person. Each area of study offers opportunity for personal growth through its own distinctive nature and process.

Movement itself is the vehicle of all programmes of study within Physical Education. Development occurs in two ways: through the mode and through the context of the movement.

The term 'mode' indicates the *manner* of the movement. Each action has its own dynamic created by the speed, strength and general ease or flow of the movement. This combines with the spatial form of the action to create the particular nature of the movement. Teachers and students talking about movement have frequently said that it is 'expressive' and we do often interpret mood from the everyday movements that we see performed around us. If a child slumps down collapsing into a chair with a heavy movement we might construe tiredness or a dispirited mood. In drama the manner of movement is used to convey character and mood. Not only can movement convey feeling, but different bodily movements create in us a range of feelings. Recall an experience of feeling exhilarated through movement. Running freely in an open space or of rolling down a grassy bank in childhood might be such an experience. A three year old was recently seen running from tree to tree in a large park and becoming increasingly excited and elated through the activity. The running continued until he fell down in laughter and the activity was repeated several times, apparently for the sheer pleasure of the movement and the 'game'. Movement has an affective dimension: it can create and convey emotion and yet it is always performed in a context and each context will give its own quality to the experience.

The 'context' of the movement is the situation in which it is experienced. Each context has its own language, social construct and emotional tone. The different programmes of study within Physical Education introduce varied movement situations. Consider for instance, the challenge of participating in an invasion game such as unihoc or hockey. Throughout the game the player tries to make appropriate contact with the ball and contribute to defending or scoring a goal. Contrast this with the feeling of creating and performing an individual gymnastic floor sequence. The emotional tone of the context may be related to the nature of the activity we engage in or it may be dominated by the interpersonal experience through movement. Within a Physical Education lesson the child will have a range of quite different interactions with the teacher and peers. The nature and the social situation of the activity create the context.

Through movement the child interacts with others and with the environment. However, movement is more than an interactive medium: it is also integrating. Through the movement experience within the Physical Education lesson we engage the affective, interpersonal and cognitive dimensions of the child.

Dance lessons can provide opportunity to increase the movement vocabulary and foster skilful use of the body. They may also give the chance to practise the skills of decision-making and problem-solving, as well as contributing to the development of aesthetic judgment. Cognitive activity is associated with dance through discussion of the stimulus and ideas as well as through the appreciation of dance works. Working with others can significantly contribute to the development of personal confidence. Sherborne (1990) contends that in order to live successfully in society children need to feel comfortable in their own bodies and to be able to make effective relationships. Dance, through its non-verbal communication and working with other dancers, enables the development of interpersonal sensitivity and the ability to relate to others. It is important that children are placed in the position of having to work in movement and respond through observation and sensitivity to each

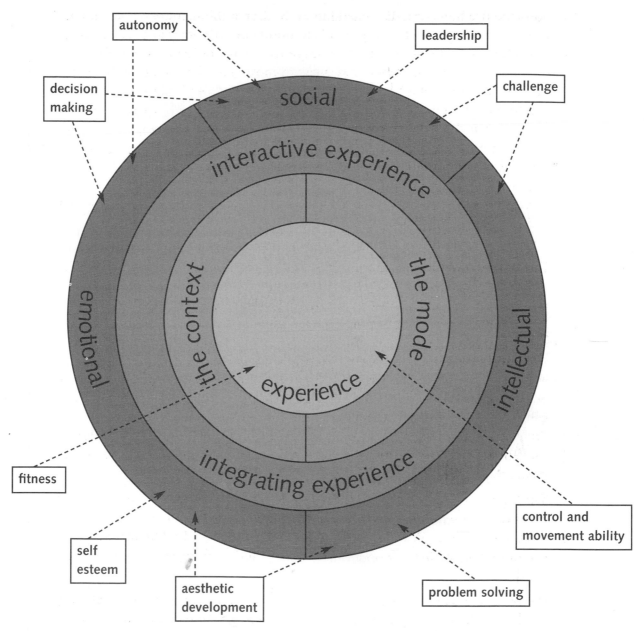

- The **mode** of movement indicates the style and form of movement in the different activities.
- The **context** is the situation in which movement is experienced and this could be any aspect of the lesson, a dance performance, gymnastic work or a game. Each activity or context has its own construct and emotional tone.
- Through movement the child **interacts** with the environment and with others.
- Movement can be an **integrating** experience touching emotional, social and intellectual aspects of the being.

Figure 1.1 *Dance and the development of the child*

other. This experience is significantly different to the negotiation which takes place as groups discuss and make decisions about their dance, or engage in evaluation of work.

DANCE IN THE THE NATIONAL CURRICULUM

Between 1987 and 1997 the development of the National Curriculum for Physical Education has resulted in a number of published statements which have articulated good practice in Physical Education. The 1992 Non-Statutory Guidance, the revised 1995 Curriculum and subsequent Exemplification of Standards material is all valuable to the teacher of dance. Curriculum review and educational change will continue but this text relates in particular to the 1995 curriculum statement.

The Attainment Target

Within the National Curriculum for Physical Education the teacher's management of the lesson will lead the child to the processes of the attainment target, planning, performing and evaluating the physical activity. The Physical Education Attainment Target requires that children should be involved in the continuous process of **planning, performing and evaluating**.

The General Requirements

Through the experience of the lessons, dance has the potential to contribute to each of the three General Requirements for Physical Education at Key Stages 1 and 2 of the National Curriculum (1995).

Dance contributes to the general requirements of the National Curriculum for Physical Education

- 1a Dance involves physical activity
- 1b Dance emphasises body awareness leading to good posture and appropriate body use
- 1c Dance involves cardiovascular and flexibility activities
- 2b Children may be confronted by their limitations in composing movements they can execute
- 2c They will be involved in consolidating performance as dances are formed
- 2d They will work in relationship with others
- 3e They can learn to prepare and cool down at the end of the session

Dance and Fitness

Dance has a contribution to make to the fitness of the child. Flexibility is promoted through the initial stretching, and aerobic activity is experienced through the locomotor warm-up or step pattern work. Through the appropriate teaching strategies the children can come to understand the effect of exercice on the body. Even more important, dance has the potential to encourage a child's sensitivity to his or her body. The child who learns body awareness may be better able to recognise inappropriate muscle tension, poor posture or other detrimental use of the body later in life.

The Programme of Study

The lesson content will deliver the programme of study at both Key Stages.

Key Stage 1	Key Stage 2
a to develop control, co-ordination, balance, poise and elevation in the basic actions of travelling, jumping, turning, gesture and stillness.	a to compose and control their movements by varying shape, size, direction, level, speed, tension and continuity.
b to perform movements or patterns, including some from existing dance traditions.	b to perform a number of different dance forms from different times and places, including some traditional dances of the British Isles.
c to explore moods and feelings and to develop responses to music through dance by using rhythmic responses and contrasts of speed, shape, direction and level.	c to express feelings, moods and ideas. to respond to music, and to create simple characters and narratives through dance in response to a range of stimuli.

Table 1.1 *The programmes of study for dance*

Physical Education and dance may be differently expressed in a revised National Curriculum, but the essential processes and content do not change. The contribution to the development of the child has so far been related to the essential nature of the activity, but dance can also contribute to the teaching of other subjects. There are many examples of this contextual use of dance in the following pages.

DANCE AS AN ART FORM

Within Physical Education only dance is an art form, and only the dance programme of study offers the child the opportunity to function as an artist. This involves experiencing the creative process through making dances, performing them and developing appreciation of the art through looking at dance and evaluating the work.

Much has been written about the nature of the arts but there are three key features of artistic work:

- artists have a specific intention to communicate through the work of art
- the work is consciously formed or made
- it is the expression of the artists' response to some aspect of their world.

The dance can be created as a response to experience and so through dance, we can give children an opportunity to relate to their own experience and environment.

Mature artists function with skill, and work with feeling, to communicate to others through their chosen art form. Dancers have movement knowledge and bodily skill to work with in creating the performance. Choreographers put emotional energy and something of their being into the work, making a personal statement. Both choreographer and dancer become vulnerable when the dance is performed for others to see and respond to. This personal involvement with the subject may be a reason for some teachers putting dance aside, while others may have concerns about lack of knowledge or skill. The very nature of the arts means that there are similarities between dance, music and the visual arts. All of these subjects can be approached by the generalist teacher with some understanding of the medium and the rules of the form.

To deliver the dance curriculum the teacher needs:

- movement knowledge
- understanding of the process of making dances.

In the past there may have been the notion that the arts are the province of the specialist, the patron, the artist and the connoisseur. Today through the work of such bodies as the Arts Council, there is a change from the purely elitist access to art. The sense of community art is growing, reflected in the increasing number of community dance workers and animateurs who bring dance within the reach of the children we teach. There is also more opportunity to look at dance through the popular media where children may see a variety of dance forms. Figure 1.2 illustrates the varied dance forms which have existed and are still found within society. It emphasises the ongoing evolution of dance. It also reminds us that dance is an activity for all people.

Dance has lived across the cultures of different times and countries. It has been a part of ritual and the recreation of the people. People dance for pleasure – the pleasure of moving and of being caught up in the rhythm of dance.

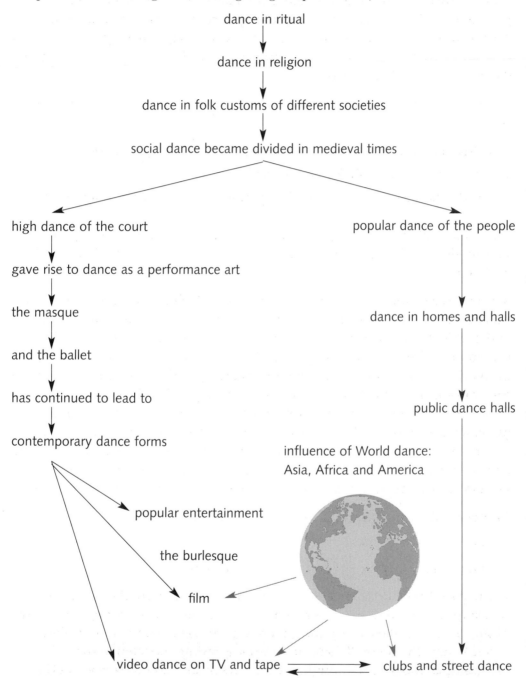

This diagram is not drawn to a time-scale and cannot represent the history of World dance but it does illustrate some of the ways that dance has existed and evolved in our society

Figure 1.2 *Dance in society*

In dance, as in other arts, the established forms change in a continuing process. Today, modern or contemporary dance exists alongside traditional ballet, and the forms continue to influence each other and evolve. Styles of dance reflect the culture of their origins, but artists can also use their art to challenge that culture. An art form is in a perpetual state of change and evolution. It is important to acknowledge the one constant feature of this particular art form; it is created in and lives through *movement.*

The dual location of dance within both the Physical Education curriculum and the expressive arts domain should not be seen as conflicting but as complementary. In its early years, during the mid 1950s and 60s, dance within education matched the child-centered mood of the time because of its emphasis on the pupil creating and expressing. Perhaps because of the emphasis on the expressive nature of dance, initially the teaching was much concerned with the movement knowledge and the expression of feeling. Since its introduction into the primary school, curriculum dance has become an academic discipline in its own right with secondary school examinations and tertiary degree courses. The development of dance throughout all phases of education has clarified the nature of the subject and the discipline now puts emphasis on three processes: making, performing and appreciating. As teachers we must be concerned with all three activities. The nature and processes of the dance fulfill the requirement of the National Curriculum to plan, perform, and evaluate.

● The processes of Dance and the PE attainment target

PE requires that children should be involved in the continuous process:

- planning
- performing
- evaluating

The dance tradition is one of:

- making
- performing
- appreciating

► THE PROCESS OF DANCE AND DANCE TEACHING

Dance offers children the opportunity to develop:

- understanding of movement
- awareness and control of the moving body

- experience of the creative process in making dances
- experience and enjoyment of performing
- appreciation of the art through looking at dance and valuing work.

The teacher's role is to help the child dance and create dances, therefore both teacher and child are engaged in the creative process. The teacher becomes a facilitator for the child as an artist.

● The creative process within the arts

There are several stages in the development of a piece of work.

- Responding to a stimulus
- Experimenting with movement
- Selecting movements to go into the dance
- Forming the dance
- Reviewing and perhaps reforming the dance
- Performing
- Receiving the appraisal and appreciation of those who see the dance.

Responding to a stimulus This may mean talking with your class in the classroom. There can be two phases. *interpretations*

First the interpretation of the symbol, which requires questions such as:

What does the stimulus mean?

How does it make me feel ?   *Brainstorming stage.*

What do we want to say through our dance?

This leads to the second stage, about the movement content of the dance :

What movement do we need?

How shall we move?

Initially you may be asking key questions but children can be surprising in their readiness to bring stimulus and **suggestions for interpretation.**

Experimenting with movement This stage takes place in the dance lesson when children have an opportunity to try out different ways of moving. *Experimental stage.*

Selecting movements to go into the dance It is essential that children learn that they can and must make decisions and choose what goes into the final work. At Key Stage 1 the teacher may need to structure the choice but the experience of selecting is an important one and should begin early.

Forming the dance means moving from improvisation and experiment to a known start and sequence of movements. With younger children, and initially at Key Stage 2, the teacher may structure the dance but the children can learn this skill.

Reviewing and perhaps reforming the dance is more likely to begin at Key Stage 2 as children look critically at work in progress.

Performing does not always mean performing in front of a special or invited audience, although this can have its place. It is important to perform for the enjoyment of the finished work and as a recognition of the achievement – it is, after all, a performance art and happens in a dimension of time.

Receiving the appraisal and appreciation of those who see the dance. In encouraging children to look at and appraise dances we develop their appreciation of the art form and this is a significant contribution to their education.

The creative process and the discipline of the dance place demands on the teacher. Not all teachers feel that they have a gift, aptitude or the confidence for teaching dance and yet class teachers have to deliver this aspect of the curriculum at Key Stages 1 and 2. This is possible if we analyse and understand the knowledge and process which will be used.

In order to create in dance the child needs:

- movement experience
- a stimulus to respond to
- time to experiment
- opportunity to create.

Within a sequence of lessons the teacher needs

- to promote bodily knowledge of movements with which to make dances
- to allow time to experiment and improvise
- to help select appropriate movements
- to help in forming the dance
- to provide the occasion to perform it.

All this can be delivered through the structuring of the lesson and the use of appropriate and varied teaching styles.

As you read through this book you may feel that the same actions are suggested and used with many different dance ideas. The reality is that children need many opportunities to practise the basic locomotor and movement skills. Dance ideas allow us to provide many different contexts for that essential practice. Perhaps it is helpful to use the analogy of reading: children do not learn to read from one book but gain the skill slowly through many and varied interactions with books; so with dance, the same actions are refined through repeated use. If we consider work in the visual arts there are other parallels: the colour, line and texture in painting, for example, may compare with the shape and dynamics of action in dance. In visual art and dance, basic components are used in varied ways to make different pictures, or dances.

Dance is an exciting subject to teach. The processes outlined in this chapter and developed in the book will come alive when children come to tell you that they have an idea for a dance or tell you that they have made a dance and ask to show it to you. This can happen surprisingly quickly.

Starting points: what do we teach and where do we start?

The chapter reviews the movement knowledge we work with, the process of selecting appropriate movement material from a stimulus, the action tasks needed to develop movement skill and the structuring of the dance. It concludes with a focus on the lesson.

DEVELOPING MOVEMENT KNOWLEDGE

Movement knowledge is both physical and verbal and, in order to effectively deliver the National Curriculum, both of these ways of knowing must be fostered. As adults we have considerable movement knowledge but we may have become unaware of it, taking our everyday movement ability for granted. We may have become restricted to the use of particular patterns or activities and perhaps teaching will reintroduce us to parts of our vocabulary that we seldom use in our daily lives. If we are to develop both children's ability to move well and their understanding of movement it is essential that we can talk about it. Every lesson is transacted through words. Teachers need the vocabulary to set movement tasks for the class as well as the language to discuss the work in progress.

For the children the experience of physical movement increases bodily knowledge, and the acquisition of a spoken movement vocabulary facilitates the oral element of the evaluation process which is required by the Physical Education attainment target.

Movement knowledge can be described in different ways and Laban's analysis in terms of body, space, dynamics and relationship, has been used to underpin physical education since the 1960s. It offers a generic understanding helpful in establishing the broad movement vocabulary of the Key Stage 1 phase. It is not the only analysis, and other frameworks give helpful descriptors for the games related manipulative activity.

Movement Knowledge consists of learning about:

- the body we live in and move with
- the space we move through
- the dynamic quality and the energy of the movement we make
- the relationship established and experienced through movement.

The body

Observation of the moving body answers the questions:

What is moving?

What activity is performed?

- Body awareness means helping children gain a sense of their own body. This enables increased control and through this, the ability to enjoy moving. Body awareness also involves developing a sensitivity to the flow of movement through the body.
- Body activity identifies the actions made or used in a dance. These may be actions of the whole body such as travelling, or actions of a single body part such as a turn of the head.

The space

Study of the space answers the questions:

Where is the movement being performed?

What is the shape or pattern of the movement in the space?

- Awareness of spatial areas means helping the child to work in the shared space of the room and the personal space immediately round the body. Moving in different directions and at different levels helps develop the sense of space.
- Spatial actions such as reaching up or going back, take the dancer into different spatial areas.
- Through an awareness of the shape of a movement and pathways in the space a child can develop a sense of pattern. This can lead to the development of motif, a repeated movement pattern or form in a dance.

The dynamic quality of movement

Looking at the dynamics of the activity answers the question:

How does the person move?

- Through exploration of the three aspects of time, strength and flow of movement, the vocabulary is enriched.

- Use of dynamics is an important element of communication through movement. The experience of different qualities can create different feeling or emotion in the dancer.

Relationship through movement

Relationship grows out of an activity. It is the interaction between people or between an individual and the environment.

- Each form of relationship creates a distinct interpersonal experience with others. Following, leading, going together or being surrounded, all give quite different feelings.

- The relationship with other dancers or objects in the space leads to formation.

- Relationship also exists in time with dancers moving in unison, canon, or taking turns to respond to each other.

It is important for the physically-educated child that movement knowledge is kinaesthetic as well as cognitive. This means that movement must be known as a bodily experience. The child as dancer may think and talk about movement and there is a cognitive dimension to the world of dance but in teaching it must be the embodied knowledge which is of paramount importance. This can be a challenge to those teachers who feel they have no movement knowledge or who do not themselves enjoy moving. Using movement words can be a way to approach dance teaching. Combinations of words can lead to simple movement phrases and into dances, or the focus on words can help children respond to a stimulus and decide on the movements they need in their dance. Charts of movement words can be introduced into the classroom and the dance workspace. Children can contribute their own words and the charts can become a language teaching resource when writing about dance. It is possible to create a 'wall of words' for the dance you are working on. The movement charts can be copied or adapted for use in the classroom or in the dance lesson.

photocopy

Body	Space
Body awareness: what moves	Where the body moves
– stillness and movement – use of the whole body – use of individual body parts – fingers, feet, elbows, knees, shoulders, head, torso – body shape: thin, wide, round twisted, big, small, symmetric and asymmetric – simultaneous/successive movement through the body	– awareness of the self in the whole working space – use of the space around the body, the person space – size: big and small, body shape and movements – pathways: straight and curved lines on the floor and in the air – levels: low, medium, high – directions: backwards, forwards, sideways, changing directions – pattern in movement – spatial actions, the bodily action and feeling of: going up and down going backwards and forwards going sideways
Body activities: what the body does	
– stillness and movement – locomotion: walk, run, roll, slide, skip – jumping: different ways of jumping, on two feet, on one foot etc. – turning: different ways of turning – expanding and contracting, growing and shrinking, bending, stretching, rolling – gesture: movement without weight transfer	

Dynamics	Relationships
The dynamic quality of movement: how the body moves	The relationship experience: going together, leading and following, meeting and parting, acting and responding, surrounding and supporting or being surrounded and supported
Time – fast, quick, sudden, speedy movement – slow, sustained movement with a sense of endlessness Weight – strong or heavy movement – light and gentle movement Flow – continuous, flowing movement with momentum, which can be hard to stop – controlled movement which can be stopped at any moment Space – bodily movements may have a single spatial focus in one direction with the whole body involved – movements may also demonstrate an awareness of different parts of the body becoming sinuous and multifaceted Work on rhythm and sequencing arises from the study of dynamic quality.	In space – moving alone in the space – moving with a partner or in a group – the whole class moving together or individually to the teacher – this may lead to moving in formations and patterns with others in the group In time – moving in unison, sequence or question and answer form

Figure 2.1 *Movement knowledge*

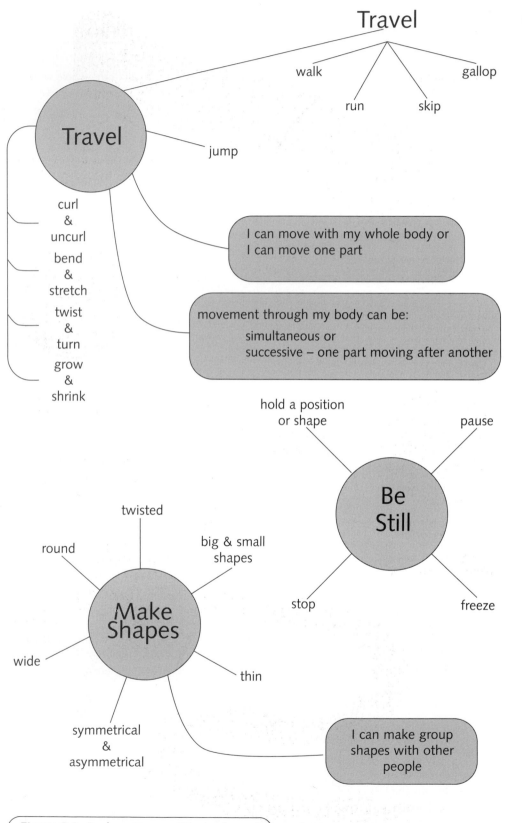

Figure 2.2 *Body actions – 'My body can'*

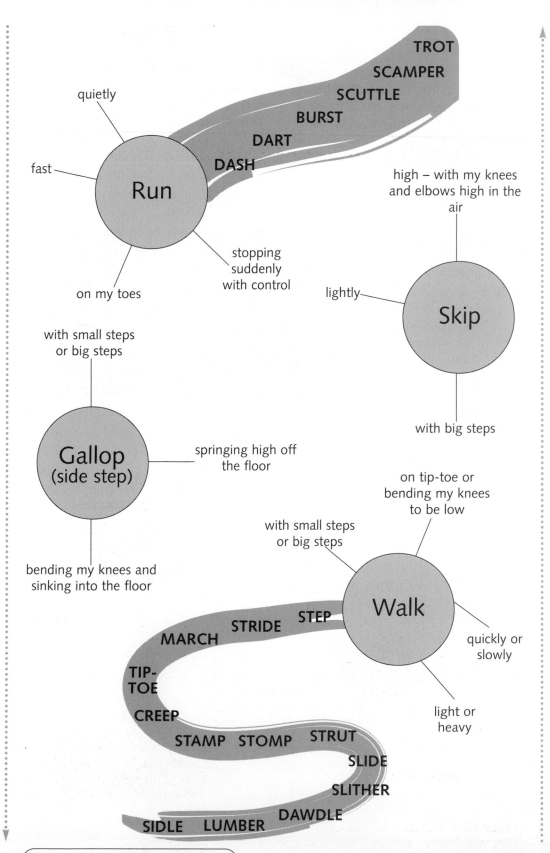

Figure 2.3 *Travelling on my feet*

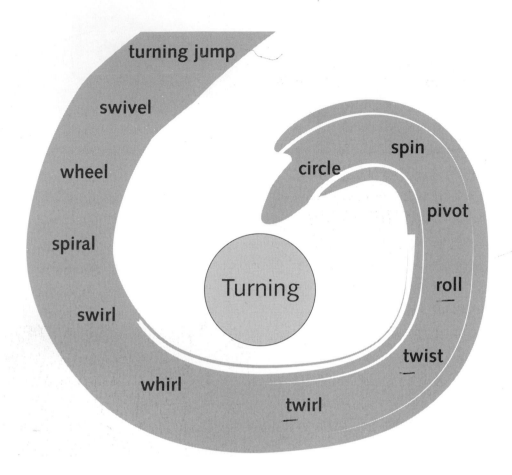

turning jump

swivel

wheel

spiral

swirl

whirl

twirl

circle

spin

pivot

roll

twist

Turning

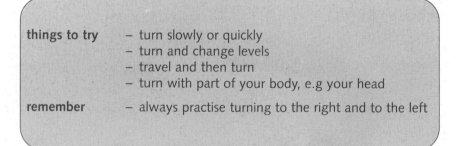

things to try	– turn slowly or quickly
	– turn and change levels
	– travel and then turn
	– turn with part of your body, e.g your head
remember	– always practise turning to the right and to the left

Figure 2.4 *Turning*

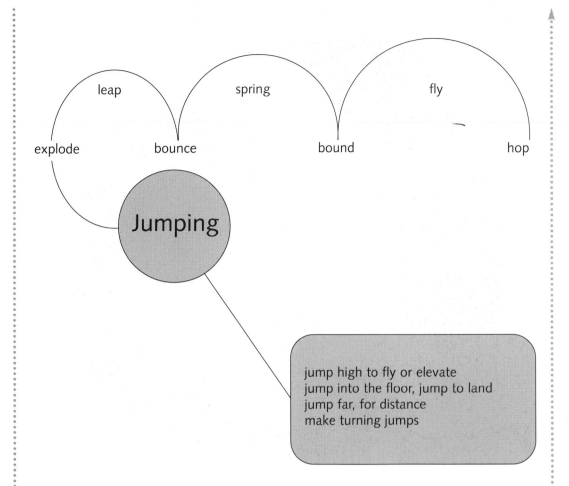

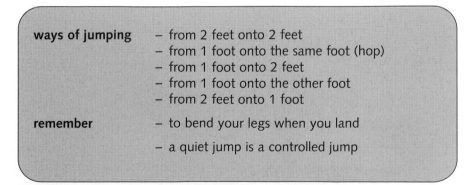

Figure 2.5 *Jumping*

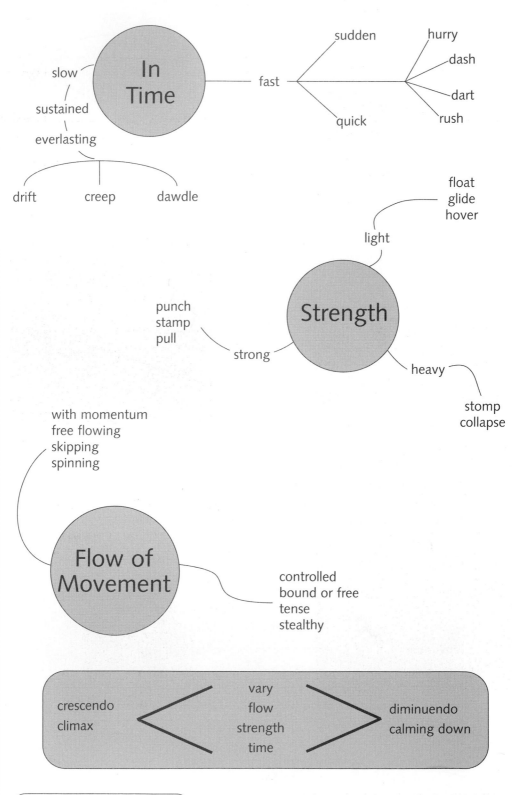

Figure 2.6 *How we move*

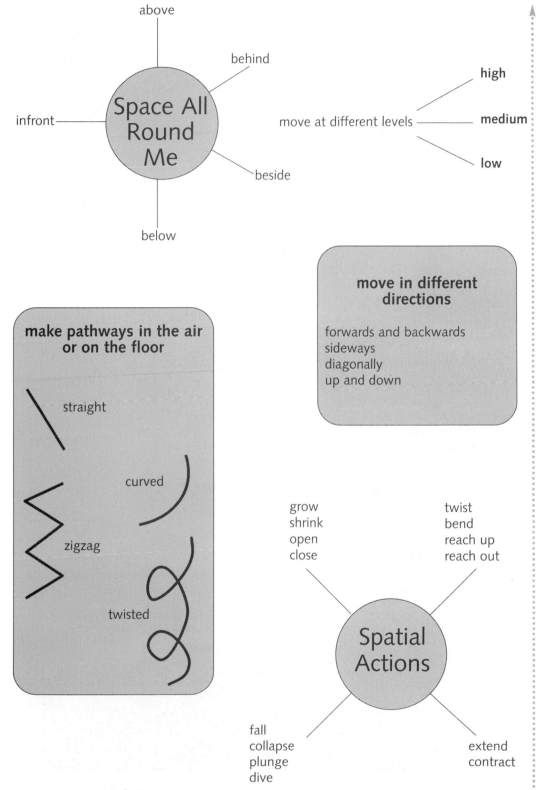

Figure 2.7 *The space we move in*

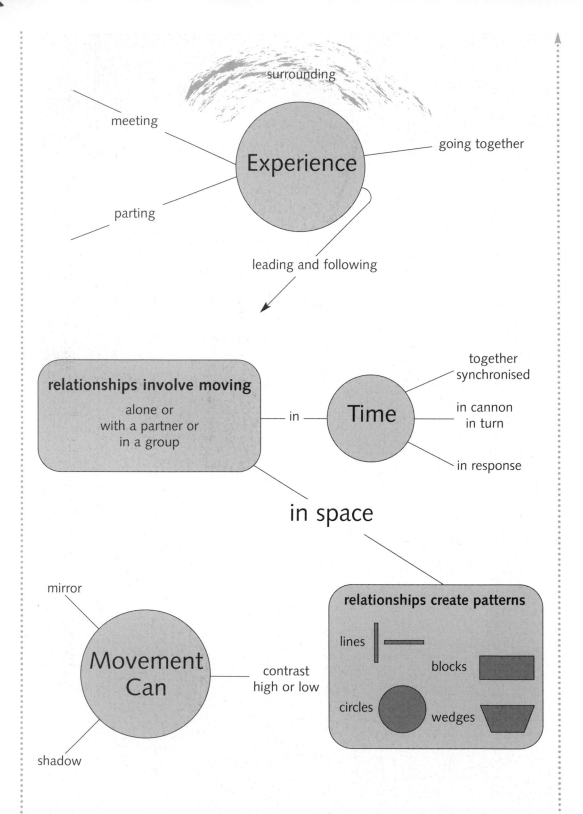

Figure 2.8 *Relationship*

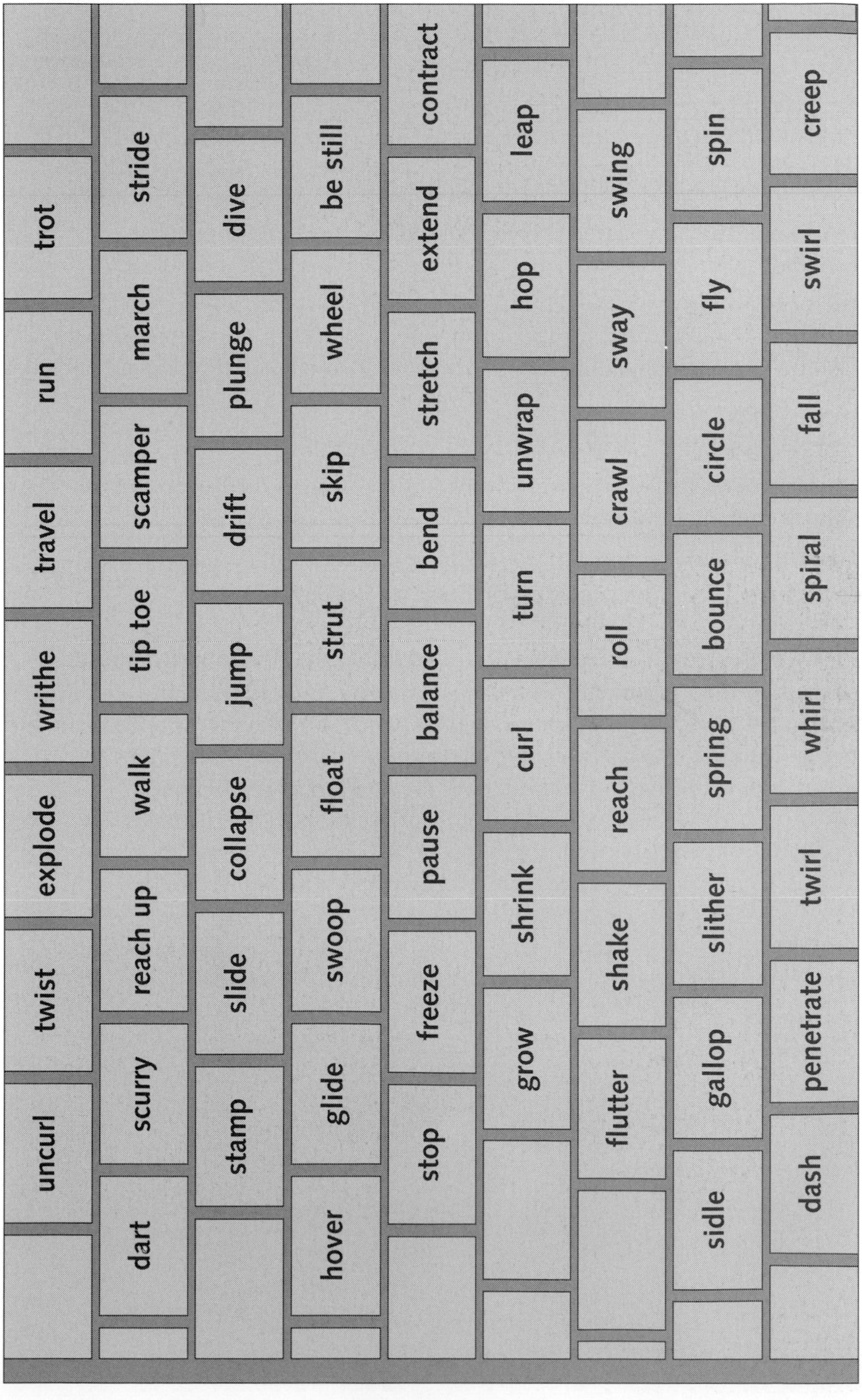

Figure 2.9 *A wall of movement words*

uncurl, twist, explode, writhe, travel, run, trot

dart, scurry, reach up, walk, tip toe, scamper, march, stride

stamp, slide, collapse, jump, drift, plunge, dive

hover, glide, swoop, float, strut, skip, wheel, be still

stop, freeze, pause, balance, bend, stretch, extend, contract

grow, shrink, curl, turn, unwrap, hop, leap

flutter, shake, reach, roll, crawl, sway, swing

sidle, gallop, slither, spring, bounce, circle, fly, spin

dash, penetrate, twirl, whirl, spiral, fall, swirl, creep

► FROM MOVEMENT TO DANCES

Dances can be generated from a wide range of different ideas or stimuli but three broad categories are particularly useful in primary education:

- dances derived from movement ideas or themes;

for example, a dance based on levels or a dance using different ways of travelling;

- dances from stimulus which may be an object, a poem, a piece of music or related to a classroom topic; for example, a dance on the theme of water. Some of these dances may have a narrative element but they will not all tell a story.

- dances related to specific cultures or dance forms;

for example, a dance inspired by Indian music, dances leading to English country dancing or to some other folk or historic dance form.

Selecting the movement content of the lesson

Whatever the stimulus or dance idea, the teacher and the pupils should be clear about the movement vocabulary of the lesson. By introducing action tasks which will allow the children to experience different kinds of movement, then promoting practice so that they move with control, the teacher can provide the vocabulary which will allow the child to create in dance.

Figures 2.10, 2.11 and 2.12 *In Key Stage 1 dance contributes to the development of basic locomotor skills such as marching, creeping and jumping*

Dances from movement ideas

Dances based on simple movement ideas can help to develop the child's movement vocabulary. The movement charts can help to suggest the content for these dances.

Examples: Body

- *Develop a simple travelling dance from the actions bounce, march, creep and skip [for reception/year 1 children]*

Practise each action with percussion and sequence the final dance with percussion accompaniment; for example, bounce alone in the space, march in and out of other people, repeat this sequence; add skip in and out of other people, and then creep, repeat this before ending with skipping. Children can be encouraged to tell the story of the dance

> *We jumped and bounced in the space, we marched, we crept towards our teacher then we skipped away.*

Figure 2.13 *Year 3 children continue to work on body awareness and control in movement. These children concentrate on using their feet and knees to make a controlled landing.*

● **Dance for bounce march creep and skip**

movement practice	teaching points
sitting – shake ankles & stop – 'floppy feet' – standing – shake hands high up or low down stretch up slowly & down	– listening to tambour for start & stop

- stepping to the tambour stepping in different directions
- marching – lifting knees high marching in different directions
- bouncing – practise jumping 2 to 2
- creeping – practise creeping with small steps – practise creeping on your toes making the dance –
- listen to the sounds and tell me which action goes to each sound
- practise – bounce, march, skip, creeping actions
- talk about space – bounce on the spot and march in and out of others
- repeat this sequence of bounce & march
- skip in and out of others then creep

teaching points:
- suggest different directions
- tambour – coach soft & bouncy knees
- if necessary stand on toes
- percussion – watch for space
- coach use of in & out of others

final dance –
- bounce & march repeated
- skip, creep & skip
- perform dance

teaching points:
- coach use of space – play sequence again
- if time perform in half class groups and evaluate with the children

● *Develop a simple dance from the actions stretch, shrink, turn and travel. [KS2]*

Practise the actions with an emphasis on the use of the space and the body shapes created. Make a sequence of stretch and shrink. Develop this using three different extended shapes; add a turning action. Try to repeat the sequence at a different level. Find a way to travel to a new place and repeat your stretching and turning motif. This dance can be developed by working with a partner to make a pair dance. *Music:* use slow music such as 'Chi Mai', by Ennio Morricone.

● Dance for stretch, shrink, turn travel

movement practice	teaching points
● extend & contract – twice	– look for body shape, symmetry or asymmetry
● on floor – extend, contract & roll to new position	– look for shape & continuity of movement flow
● extend on 3 points e.g. 2 feet & 1 hand	– practise balance on 2 feet & 1 hand & look at use of space & extension of body
● standing – bounce & spring	– coach resilience (knees)
● travel – side step or gallop leap & run & leap & leap	– tambourine – use of space – look for extension of feet
● travel & turning jump standing	– travel, jump, turn
● extend & contract practise varied dynamics out slowly & back quickly out quickly & back slowly	– look for stretch through whole body – percussion to support action
● task – sequence – extend, contract, 3 times & add a turn	– time to practise 3 mins, check – use of whole body movement never stops (flow)
● this is your movement pattern (motif) practise it again, then try it at a low level	– look for flow of movement
● find partner – observe half class	– watch your partner – look for quality of stretch & curl
● repeat task – other person observe	– look at pattern, is there contrast in the shape used?
● in pairs we are going to work together without talking but by watching your partner – dance your sequence near your partner	
	– do you dance at the same level?
repeat task – try to be more aware of your partner, make eye contact – use the motif to start of dance,	
travel to a new place – repeat your sequences again final performance	– give time to practise
● motif – travel – repeat – motif	
● look – half class groups	– look for growing of extension, clear motifs – work with partner

Figures 2.14 and 2.15 *Reception children use fingers high and low as they gain spatial awareness.*

Examples: Space

- *Make a dance from a visual pattern [KS1&2]* Dances can be made from spatial words but visual stimuli can also be explored. All age groups can respond to a visual pattern or pathway. The pattern can be drawn in the air, walked and travelled in different ways before making a sequence of using several ways to travel the pattern. Dances can be accompanied by percussion played by the teacher or a partner.

● **Movement tasks to help children make dances**

- working alone

– draw your pattern in the air

– walk your pattern on the floor

– run, hop or skip pattern on the floor

– find three ways to travel your pathway.

- KS 1

– music e.g. Scott Joplin Rag – choose a clear starting position – high or low, travel your pathway and have a clear ending, high or low.

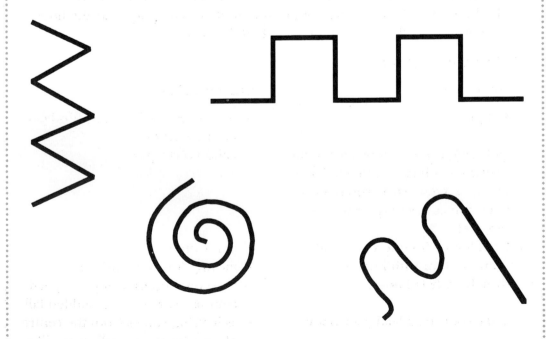

Figure 2.16 *Visual patterns as dance stimuli*

- KS 2

– travel pathway and have speed contrast

– travel pathway and have change in levels

– travel pathway and introduce rhythmic element

– develop individual sequence.

- Older KS 1 & KS 2

- working with a partner

– show partners your dance – learn your partners dance – follow your partner

– choose partner with a different pathway – learn both pathways – decide which part of your dance comes first

– develop individual sequence and partner provides percussion accompaniment

develop pair dance with music as above

develop the work as a group piece

– the objective may be – to develop a sequence from using stimuli but equally it may be to produce sequence with clear spatial and dynamic quality.

- *Make a high and low dance with a Key Stage 1 class* Fingers can drum on the floor, reach upwards and fall down again. Elbows, hands and head can take it in turns to lead the body from the floor up towards the ceiling, and children can walk tall on tip toes, travel low down creeping near the floor, or skip, getting the knees and elbows high in the air.

● Dance for high & low

movement practice	teaching points
skipping	– use of space – in & out of others use percussion
galloping & go to floor on stopping, stretching – fingers, stretch & curl arms, stretch & curl, whole body, stretch & curl, sitting stretch & flex feet	– gallop & drop
from low or floor level, to high draw on floor with fingers stretch up & fall down	– percussion – moving finger round you – try several times & enjoy – speed contrast, slow stretch, sudden fall
make your head lead your body	– as if string comes from the centre of your head and pulls you – like a puppet being pulled up

make your elbows lead your body

- travelling – on tip-toes – walk   – look for balance – think about
  on tip-toes – skip   your whole body
  walk low creeping   – bend knees low – what shape is
                                           your whole body?

form the dance

- from the floor fingers or elbows lead   – choose – will you use fingers or
  up & fall 3 times   elbow? show me
  skipping in & out of others   – elbows & knees high
  creeping low, near floor   – may creep to centre & skip away
  whole body stretches & shrinks,
  springs up high to end
- talk sequence through   – help children recall sequence
  play sound through
  possibly decide on pathway – creep
  to centre & skip out
- perform dance

- *At Key Stage 2 a sequence of pathways in the air* can be developed into a simple dance with a partner acting as a mirror. *Music:* 'Cavatina', by Myers, played by John Williams.

● Tasks for a dance on pathways in the air

task	teaching points
- make a pattern of circles in the space	– use the whole body, look for good weight transfer
in front of you beside you above you	
- make a pattern of straight lines include a change in levels	– as above & look at quality of extension in starting position
- make a pattern of straight and curved lines a motif make motif small make motif large draw motif with head draw motif with hand	
in pairs – look at motifs or patterns & use of levels	– is there good use of whole body?
in pairs – learn both patterns & perform them in a sequence	
in pairs – work as a pair & create new pattern	

decide – does the dance need travel?
or how does dance end?

Examples: Dynamics

- *At Key Stage 1 a simple fast and slow dance* might be sequenced from such activities as: growing slowly into a shape then changing body shape suddenly, creeping slowly can be contrasted with sudden jumping and travelling fast and freezing before turning round slowly and repeating the movement phrase.

● **Tasks for a fast and slow dance**

tasks	teaching points
● shoot out into the space & curl up slowly	– percussion or tambour
● uncurl slowly & shrink suddenly	
● slowly grow into a shape & hold it change shape and hold the new shape change again & make your shape at a different level	
● slowly creep into space creep slowly & suddenly look behind	– develop rhythmic phrase e.g. creep, creep & jump
● skipping in the space	
● spinning on the spot – fast	

ideas for forming the dance
- stretch & shrink – fast & slow
- skipping & stop in shape
- change shape slowly
- creep in & out of others
- suddenly run & stop
- suddenly jump & end – high or low

suggestion for forming a group dance
- A – half class in centre – form a shape & then slowly change shape
- B – other half of the class – dance around and towards the centre group e.g.creeping towards slowly and suddenly jumping away groups change roles

- *At Key Stage 2* individual and partner dances can be made through responding to a set of contrasting words such as creep, pounce and dash. Using simple percussion to accompany a partner's dance can help in developing the time and strength contrasts. Children can enjoy creating word sequences for their dance lesson. The only rule is that they must have contrast. Words such as bounce, stretch and collapse offer spatial and dynamic contrast.

Figures 2.17 and 2.18   *Children experience the contrasting dynamics of stiff, jerky controlled movements performed in a stable position in a dance about machines, and the twisting, turning and tipping off balance of a dance inspired by autumn winds.*

Figures 2.19 and 2.20 *Using contact and the experience of pushing against a partner can help to develop an awareness of strong movement. [Figure 2.19]*
Children at Key Stage 2 will progress to the use of two motion factors in a single action. [Figure 2.20] These children use strength and suddenness as they approach their partner.

Suggestion/planning task Use the wall of movement words to create sets of three contrasting movement words which can be displayed as a stimulus for a movement sequence or dance.

Teaching the elements of movement knowledge develops a vocabulary of actions for children to create with. Sometimes a stimulus helps in this process. For example, in the autumn, conkers offer the contrast of the roundness of the nut inside a spiky case. This might lead to a dance about round and spiky body shapes suitable for a young class. Stimuli can be verbal, visual, tactile or musical.

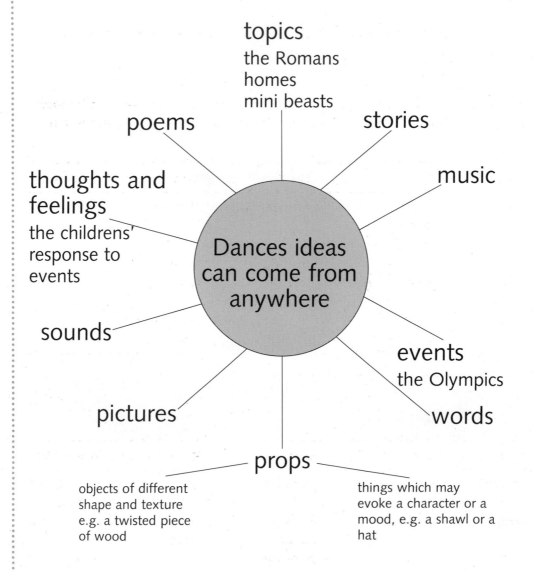

topics
the Romans
homes
mini beasts

poems

stories

music

thoughts and feelings
the childrens' response to events

Dances ideas can come from anywhere

sounds

events
the Olympics

pictures

words

props
objects of different shape and texture e.g. a twisted piece of wood

things which may evoke a character or a mood, e.g. a shawl or a hat

Figure 2.21 *Where do dance ideas come from? What makes a dance?*

The following process may help you in selecting the movement material relevant to a stimulus.

Consider the stimulus, identify key words and answer the following questions:

- How does the body move?

  What is the appropriate action ?
- How does the body move in the space or where does it go?

  What spatial knowledge is relevant?
- How is the movement performed?

  What dynamic quality should be used?
- What relationship experience is suggested?

Look at the movement charts with the children to answer these questions.

● Example: a balloon

Watching the balloon inflate, fly round the room as it is released, or bounce gently when fully inflated, this suggests the following words and movement material.

Word	Body	Space	Dynamics	Relationship
grow	extend expand round body	low to high	rhythmic	alone
fly	travel	pathways	speed	
bounce	step	levels pathways	light	
burst	fall collapse	low	sudden heavy	

Table 2.1 *Movement chart: a balloon*

● Example: snow

Word	Body	Space	Dynamics	Relationship
footprints	stepping	pathways	strong stamping	alone or with a partner
swirling	turning	levels curved pathways	varied speed	

Word	Body	Space	Dynamics	Relationship
drifting	travelling	levels straight pathways	gently	
settling	stillness	bodyshape rounded	heavy	
freezing	stillness	angular body shape	tense stiff	
melting	descending	change of body shape	varied tension and weight	

Table 2.2

● **Example: bird flight**

Word	Body	Space	Dynamics	Relationship
glide	travel	straight	smoothly	
swoop	travel	change levels	vary speed	
hover	stepping shaking	on the spot high looking down		
drop	descend		suddenly	
dart	head or whole body	vary directions	sudden light	

Table 2.3

Suggestion/planning task Consider the topic of fireworks or fire, for example, choose appropriate descriptions or action words and then use the above model to decide what actions and movement material you will teach.

The same model may be used with a poem to help determine the movement content of the lessons.

Not all topics lend themselves to this process model. Some dances may be developed through **mimetic action**. Actions of play or work can be developed into movement patterns, or dance motifs.

Example: a dance related to the topic of explorers and particularly life on the sailing ship.

working action	dance activity
loading the cargo	lifting, carrying and placing things
hauling the sails up	pulling ropes down
pushing the capstain round	stepping & pushing
sweeping the decks	stepping & sweeping

Each activity can be turned into a repeated movement pattern which can be formed into a dance.

Turning mime into motif means:

- making the action simple

- emphasising the spatial pattern and size

- making the pattern have rhythm, or a repeated pattern in time and space. The accompaniment of simple percussion can help develop the rhythmic quality of children's work. Repetition of the relevant action words in rhythmic phrases such as 'pull, and pull, and heave' can also be an effective and supportive sound.

STRUCTURING THE LEARNING – MOVEMENT TASK SETTING

Having identified the lesson material to work with, the teacher needs the skill of task setting to enable movement experience. The skill of appropriate task setting can help both teacher and pupils. As with all planning, appropriateness is determined by the abilities, developmental stage and confidence of the children, as well as by the learning or experience the teacher seeks to promote. Clear task setting is important if the child is to be able to respond with confidence, and different types of task may be relevant to stages of the lesson.

- **Exploratory tasks** may be used in the exploration and development of movement vocabulary. For example:

  Show me ways to turn.

This is an open task which all children should be able to achieve.

  Can you find three ways to turn and show me?

This task offers the child a structured choice.

A teacher response to both of these might be to observe, select several examples of work for demonstration and then let children continue to experiment with the movement.

- **Practice tasks** can be followed when the movement content of the dance has been introduced;

For example, travel, descend and roll, or travel, turn and be still in a round shape.

Appropriate teacher response would now be to identify and comment on good body use or the smooth flow of the action.

The concept of a **movement action task** is an important one. The examples above are all clear action tasks. The child knows what activity to do although there is the potential for an individual response in the choice of how the task is fulfilled.

● **Examples of movement action tasks derived from the stimulus of snow**

stamping   make big heavy stamps as if you were stamping in the snow, practise again, think about the pattern you make, can you step in different directions?
accompaniment: percussion, drum beat

swirling   travel in and out of the space making a curved pathway, practise travelling and turning on your curved pathway, add changes of level and speed as you travel.
accompaniment: percussion, shake tambourine

drifting   travel on a straight pathway and gradually come to a stop, change levels from high to low as you travel.
accompaniment: percussion, shake tambourine

settling   travel and gradually slow down and stop, make a curved shape with your body as you stop.
accompaniment: percussion, shake tambourine

freezing   make a spiky and angular shape with your body.
accompaniment: percussion, strike a tambour or woodblock

melting   start in a spiky shape, gradually change to a round shape and sink to the floor slowly.

● **Examples of movement action tasks derived from the stimulus of bird flight**

glide   travel gently in a straight pathway and pause, practise this phrase several times and try to keep the same even speed

swoop	travel freely in the space but change levels as you move, practise again but vary the speed as you change levels
hover	pull yourself up to a tall shape and move on tip-toe, look down and move on the spot taking little steps
drop	fall suddenly to the floor, practise the action for hovering and then drop down suddenly.

All of these tasks can be accompanied with a tambourine

Suggestion/planning task Use the material of the last planning activity (page 38) to make clear action tasks for the movements related to fireworks.

- **Interpretive tasks** also have a place in dance lessons once the child is confident, having a movement vocabulary to respond with. Asking the child to improvise to the music or interpret a poem in movement can become appropriate surprisingly quickly. If the stimulus is discussed, the children can identify the movements to go into their dance using the movement charts and processes outlined.

▶ STRUCTURING THE DANCE

There are different ways in which the teacher can help children to understand and develop the ability to *form* the dance. Without form the movement experience does not become 'a dance'.

A simple dance can have three sections:

- a known start,
- a middle and
- an ending.

At Key Stage 1, it is important to establish the sense of *performing* a dance. Initially the teacher may sequence the activities giving the support of percussion and suggesting a broad spatial structure.

● **Example:**

a travelling dance

Begin with skipping freely in the space,

followed by several phrases of stepping towards the teacher and jumping away. Follow with a jumping section working on the spot, and conclude with a return to the free skipping in space.

Alternatively a number of movements can be introduced and practised in the lesson and the children can form their final dance from this vocabulary of actions. This way of working is particularly appropriate when using music. Even the youngest children can be asked to think about their first movement and have a clear start to the dance. Within the first key stage some children will recall movements and even dances from earlier lessons and others will recreate a new dance each lesson.

Careful task setting can help older children to structure their dances. Working with the movement material presented in the lesson, children can be asked to select three of the movements practised and sequence them to make a dance. It is important to allow time to experiment, to choose and then to practise the sequence.

Example A dance based on the theme of bird flight could be derived by asking the children to select three of the movements they enjoyed and sequencing them into a dance with a clear start, middle and ending. An emphasis on contrast can help the structuring. You may suggest spatial contrast such as a part of the dance travelling and a part on the spot.

Working in groups to make a dance

When asking children to build a group dance try to work through movement. Children with some experience of dance and who are confident in their movement vocabulary may be happy to improvise as a group, but talking with children has reinforced the belief that not all young people are happy to work in this way. It is important to ensure that the children have movement ideas to work with. Through the initial teaching of the lesson allow children to experiment and form their own movement patterns, or motifs. The group can then look at each motif and decide which to use. Having selected an action pattern they can then decide on the spatial formation. Structuring the process of building the dance in this way leads to a clear dance outcome.

ORGANISING AND MANAGING THE LESSON

Preparation

Preparation will include changing into appropriate clothing. There should be an expectation of working barefoot if the floor surface permits. The awareness of feet and the quality of work are significantly improved without shoes. For those who have foot infections it is important that they work in danceshoes or plimsoles and not the hefty trainers which may be appropriate to games or outdoor lessons.

As teachers we should consider our own dress; this can give the children an indication of attitude to the subject. The role and individual personality of the class teacher will be significant in determining the practice. It might be realistic to aim to teach in trackwear or to wear trousers and be prepared to change shoes or work barefoot.

Suggestion Review the practice on dress for lessons and decide what is appropriate for children and staff of your school.

The lesson

The dance lesson like all other Physical Education lessons has three stages:

- introductory activity and body preparation
- development   i   movement teaching
                       ii   application in dance
- conclusion, performance of the dance and cool down.

It is important to have two foci in the second stage. There should be time to add to or reinforce the movement skill or knowledge as well as time to create or add to the dance.

It is helpful to be specific in your planning. Identify the movement action tasks you will set and phrase them appropriately to the age range you are teaching.

Starting the lesson

The **introductory activity** is important and can:

- establish the physical nature of the lesson
- promote   aerobic activity
                      body awareness
                      flexibility
- help children to make the transition from a classroom activity to dance
- help the teacher focus the class and engage them in the lesson. A simple whole class activity can be effective in this.

● Examples

Aerobic warm up: accompaniment: any lively music with a regular beat, for example, Scott Joplin. In a whole class circle travel, walk, side-step/gallop facing inward and then outward, skip, repeating the sequence for a longer period of activity with older children.

Tasks to promote more complex step patterns:

- Travel and show me different ways of travelling on your feet.
- Make patterns of steps as you travel, for example make a pattern of running and hopping or walking and jumping.
- With a partner travel together taking turns to choose the way of travelling or make a step pattern for your partner to follow.
- Choose or make up your own step pattern and travel showing different directions, forwards, sideways etc.

Rhythmic warm up: accompaniment; tambour.

Can you take one step for every beat? Play sequences of beats of varied pace:

/ / / / / / ,   / . / . / / / / ,   /   /   /   /

Introduce patterns of stepping and pause, for example steps and a pause. Vary the rhythms:

/ / / –, / / / –,/ / / –, / / / / –, / / / / –, / / / / –, / / / / –

Introduce more complex rhythms, for example step step and jump:

/ / – / , / / – / , / / – /

Rhythmic work can have a gamelike or fun dimension. It can help children to develop a repertoire of step patterns as well as rhythmic sense. 'Can I catch you out ?' is a popular challenge.

Flexibility and body awareness warm up:

Key Stage 1

Can you gently move every part of your body? Draw circles with your shoulders? Stretch up as far as you can? Stretch out as far as you can? etc.

Sitting on the floor with legs straight out in front, stretch and flex your feet, circle your ankles. (Talk about the feeling/tension in the legs as the stretch is made.)

Key Stage 2

At this stage, a sequence of moving and stretching body parts can be worked out but it is important to remind children to stretch slowly, not to overextend until the stretch hurts, and to allow the muscle to recover after each extension before stretching again.

The warm up can revise bodily activity, and also foster body awareness. Traditionally the dance class begins with a warm up which has the pattern of:

- working on the floor,
- standing
- travelling.

Suggestion With the children develop a sequence of stretching and rolling at floor level, add a bouncing or springing activity and concentrate on awareness of knees and feet, and end with travelling.

Managing the lesson

The children can be engaged in the lesson through classroom discussion of the topic or stimulus. By sharing this they have ownership of the dance.

Clear expectations of work, and clear task-setting contribute to successful lessons. Feedback on each task is important as is the practice of stopping to look at work in progress.

Strategies for giving feedback include:

- Scan the room whilst the children are working and talk during their activity to identify and promote good work or to introduce new ideas.
- Give more specific feedback by watching one or two individuals and commenting on positive or negative features of their work. The children do not have to be identified publicly.
- Stop the lesson to look at a group of children working and give feedback from this.

Managing the space

All classes have to be encouraged to use the whole workspace effectively, and this is a particular focus of work at Key Stage 1. Like many other classroom routines good use of the workspace needs regular reminders at the start of the year but can be established as an expectation.

Teachers faced with small halls may need to be creative in the strategies they use to allow children adequate workspace. Some of the following strategies may be useful:

- Paired work: one partner observes and one performs in the less crowded work space. This can be used as children practise action phrases or as they work on the dance in progress.
- Working individually children can perform in a rolling sequence with five

or six children starting and others getting up to work as their friends end their dance. This can be a useful at the end of a lesson when a dance is in process and requires performance. This method of performing in smaller numbers can also develop decision-making and sensitivity to others as each decides when to get up and work.

- Older children making a group dance may be helped by allowing each group a turn in a larger workspace and suggesting that other groups use the time to refine individual motifs or to mark through sections of the dance, clarifying the sequence.

Ending the lesson

It is important that every dance lesson ends with the children performing their dance. This values the work achieved in the lesson and recognises the importance of dance as a created phenomenon.

The National Curriculum emphasises the need for cooling down from physical activity and this may be achieved through such activities as:

- **Relaxing**: lying on the floor, stretch and relax slowly. Do this three times before lying still to concentrate on the feeling in your body. Concentrate on letting your whole body sink into the floor.
- **Stilling the body**: stand still and make a tidy body, see that you have your feet together, your knees together. Think about the line of your spine, stand tall but relax your shoulders and do not hunch them up. Let your hands hang beside you still and not fidgetting.
- **Breathing**: standing still and tall inhale and exhale, breathing deeply.

It is important to end as the lesson begins with focus on the body, the instrument of the dancer.

The organisation of an orderly departure should be as for any other hall Physical Education lesson.

Much of this chapter has been concerned with the living reality of the theory of instructional scaffolding [Applebee, 1989]. If we are to enable children to work in dance it is important to understand the processes we engage in and be articulate about them, and to structure the learning experience for the child.

The contextual use of dance

Asked what they are teaching in dance, students and teachers will often respond by talking about the dances in terms of their stimuli rather than the dance making or performance skills. The stimulus or dance idea is often derived from work in another subject. Dance like other art forms can be used to enrich the child's experience of learning across the curriculum. This chapter examines the relationship between dance and language before going on to give dance ideas relating to the core and other foundation subjects.

DANCE AND LANGUAGE WORK

The lesson itself promotes language development in several ways. The movement activity gives the child experiential understanding of the basic vocabulary associated with actions in the space. Dance also offers the young child an opportunity to make sense of descriptive words such as 'creep', 'whirl' and 'slither'. As children evaluate and discuss work they practise oracy. This may be in a structured situation responding to particular criteria in giving feedback to a partner. (Examples of the talk involved can be found in Chapter 5, page 99.)

The exploration of stimuli also offers opportunity to discuss and express ideas. In the same way that a writing frame is supportive, so key questions can help children form their oral response.

After hearing a new piece of music children might be asked :

> *What picture comes into your head?*
> *Does the music suggest a mood, an atmosphere, or does it tell a story?*
> *What are the people doing? how do they feel? how do they move?*
> *How would you feel if you were there, and how would you move?*

The questions will obviously be specific to the class and stimulus but it is important that the oral exploration does end with a consideration of the appropriate movements for the dance.

▶ DANCE IDEAS

Using poetry

The use of poetry as a starting point for dance can lead to talking about language. Robert Southey's poem 'The Cataract of Lodore' is rich in descriptive words as he captures the sight, sound and flow of the cataract (waterfall). Poems like this may be interpreted using the process described in Chapter 2. Other poems such as 'Snow Play', below, suggest the actions through the text.

● **Dance idea KS 1: Snow Play**

Stamp, stamp, stamp, marching in the snow,
Sideways and forwards, then round in rings I go.
Scraping up the snow I make a great big heap,
I want to build a snowman, a friend for me to keep.
I smooth him and pat him to get him into shape,
And then I run and jump near him to see if he's awake.
If I stay out all night with him, I'll be frozen too,
I'll be all stiff and jerky, and make a spiky dance for you.
When the sun comes out at last, I'll go all soft and round,
I'll begin to melt away and be a puddle on the ground.

Movement practice

- stamping and marching in different directions
  stepping in lines and circles

- scraping, patting, smoothing, building actions

- stiff walking
  spiky body shape
  jerky elbows, knees, head, trunk
  jerky dance

- round body shape
  sink to the ground.

accompaniment: percussion

Working with Key Stage 2 children, the emphasis may be on the forming of the motifs or forming the dance. The poem 'A Lazy Thought' by Eve Merriam also leads to work on pace and tempo.

● A Lazy Thought
Dance idea KS 2:

There go the grown ups
To the office,
To the store.
Subway rush,
Traffic crush;
Hurry, scurry,
Worry, flurry.
No wonder
Grownups
Don't grow up
Any more.
It takes a lot
Of slow
To grow.

Eve Merriam

Movement practice	*Teaching points*
• develop motifs for different ways of travel, walk, cycle, drive, stand in a train	emphasise the size of the action, make the action rhythmic
• develop motifs for work, write, word process, tear up paper, lift and carry things, stack shelves	
• decide on the sound accompaniment, read the poem repeating some lines, pay attention to the build up of the poem, crescendo, experiment with percussion	
• decide how the dance ends.	

Poetry can also lead through dance to creative writing or making a story. The poem 'The Wrigglebug Dance' could become a focus for teaching with the movement work leading to story telling and art work.

● Dance idea Nursery/Reception
The Wrigglebug Dance

Down in the forest in the dark dark night,   Section A
Things began to move in the silver moon light.
Shivering and wriggling, slowly things awoke.
I thought I heard a whisper and then someone spoke.
He said that they were Wrigglebugs and they'd come out to play,
They like to play at jumping, then creep and run away,

> *They wriggled their middle and jumped on their feet.*   Section B
> *Sometimes they were big jumps and sometimes they were neat.*
> *They skipped and they danced all about the space*
> *And when they met a friend, they made a smiling face.*
> *Creeping and jumping, then turning all around,*   Section C
> *The Wrigglebugs were startled when they heard a sudden sound*
> *CRASH!*
>
>   Music, 'A Way' by Vangelis

Movement practice

- stretch – whole body – long, wide, asymmetrically

- shiver & shake head and shoulders awake
- find a way to wake up using stretch and wriggle
- jumping – 2–2 little, long/big, 1–1, 1–2, 2–1, 1–other, turning jumps

- skip – pathways in and out of others

- creep and run away, creep and jump, creep and turning jump

Dance form
narrative Section A – waking up (stretching)
section B – individual dance, creep and run, jump big and small, skip and stop
section C – form end – creep in to centre and jump away

Language work

Oral
What does a wrigglebug look like?
How big is it? What shape is it?
What was the forest like?

How would you feel in the forest?
How did the wrigglebugs feel when they heard the noise?
What happened next?
Written
Make a class story
Write your own story
Make a big book for literacy work
Information technology
Use the computer to draw the wrigglebugs for the book

Using pictures

Music and pictures can become a powerful stimulus to story writing particularly when accessed through dance. The dance gives the child a lived experience of the story.

● Dance idea KS 1 or 2: The Castle Door

Show a picture of an old house or a castle door whilst the children listen to music and then answer the question What is behind the door?

Use key questions from page 47 to define appropriate movement work. This is likely to be predictable in response to the mood of the music.

Music from 'Concerto for Orchestra' by Bartok

Movement practice
- creep
  creep slowly and look round suddenly
  creep slowly then dash and stop
- use high and low levels
  creep and looking high and low
  feel around as you travel
- pushing and pulling things out of the way
- run and stop
  travel and jump
  travel jump descend and roll

Dance form
a narrative with a sequence of sections, A beginning, B middle, C end
an individual dance

Using stories

Children also enjoy making dances about characters in the stories they hear or read.

● Dance idea KS 1: The Lighthouse Keeper's Lunch
Music 'Sailor's Hornpipe' (Traditional)
Movement practice
- working actions of sweeping the floor,
  polishing the lamp, painting the lighthouse,
  rowing the boat, pulling & pushing equipment

Dance form
individual dance
choose 3 actions and sequence them

● Dance idea KS 2: The Dance of the Oompa Loompas (from Charlie and the Chocolate Factory)
Music 'In the Hall of the Mountain King' from the *Peer Gynt Suite* by Grieg
Movement practice
- working actions of carrying, stirring, pouring, pushing, etc.
- forming clear movement patterns, motifs
- making group motifs
- forming the dance

This dance could be developed as a writing stimulus and tell the story of the day things went wrong in the factory.

Figures 3.1, 3.2, 3.3 and 3.4 *Year 3 children use working actions for a dance based on* Charlie and the Chocolate Factory. *Groups use varied formations including a line, a wedge, and a circle with the actions of pushing [Figure 3.1], pulling [Fgure 3.2], stirring [Figure 3.3], and pouring [Figure 3.4]. The same actions and formations could also be used in a dance portraying the preparation for a Tudor Feast.*

Using a theme as a stimulus

Many themes across the curriculum have potential to become a stimulus for dance work. The dance ideas in this chapter are developed with suggestions for learning objectives, movement practices and music. Some ideas might be integrated into different themes or topics. It is important to recognise that a single stimulus can be interpreted in different ways by individuals or classes leading to quite different dances. Some dances clearly lead to particular learning objectives, for exaple the feet and fingers dance focuses on body awareness. Other dances might be placed in one of several different units of work having the potential to lead to a variety of learning outcomes, for example the skeleton dance might be in a unit relating to body awareness and performance or to units with objectives relating to forming dance or working with others. The dance ideas may be used in single lessons, particularly some of those identified for Key Stage 1, but some will obviously lead to extended pieces of work.

Theme – myself, my body

● Dance idea KS 1: Feet & Fingers Dance

Learning objective body awareness
Music percussion accompaniment
Movement practice

- fingers drumming on floor
  shaking hands high & low
  hands close to body & stretch out
  drawing lines, circles, shapes in the air
- feet, creep, stamp, slide, skip, jump
  silent feet, sudden & slow feet

Dance form ABAB
A hands – low & high
B feet – stamp & creep
A hands – draw patterns in air
B feet – lively – free dance, skip
Note This can be a single lesson within a unit.

● Dance idea KS 2: Hands & Feet Dance

Learning objective working with others or forming dance
Music 'Clog Dance' from *La Fille Mal Gardée* by Herold arr. Lanchbery
Movement practice

- hands explore space – all round body
  hands lead actions, stretch, circle etc.
  move slowly and quickly

- feet – walk, jump, hop, skip etc.
  step patterns – make simple patterns
- partner work – go together doing the same steps
  follow partner
  go in sequence A then B
  mirror your partner

Dance form ABA

children decide focus on hands feet hands or feet hands feet

Note The same dance idea could be developed with gloves and shoes as props to create characters.

● Dance idea KS1 or 2: Skeleton Dance

Learning objectives body awareness or forming the dance
Music 'Fossils' from *Carnival of the Animals* by Saint Saens
Movement practice

- moving body parts, head up & down or sideways
  shoulders
  arms elbows, hands
  hips
  knees & legs
- vary speeds slow and fast movement
  shaking/jerking
  rhythmic action
- whole body movement, shaking, bouncing, dragging, walk

Dance form A B A C A D A

Sequence of focus on whole body and on individual body parts, for example whole body moves, head moves, whole body action, hands move, whole body action, feet, and whole body dance.

KS 2 children may make individual dances, work as pairs or groups with an expectation of the whole group having a common movement motif.

● Dance idea KS 2: Blindness

Learning objectives awareness of others
Music 'Adagio in G minor for organ and strings' by Albinoni
Movement practice

- groping, floor level
- travel on feet, feeling the way
- with partner both work eyes closed, with hand or other body contact, improvise and feel your partner moving. The dance can be formed from improvisation

Dance form A alone B partner dance, or improvisation with partner.
Note It may be possible to find a dance practitioner to lead a workshop on contact improvisation.

Theme – myself, my favourite food

● **Dance idea KS1 or 2: Spaghetti, Jelly, Bread and Popcorn Dance**

Learning objectives varied dynamics, quality of movement

Music 'Pineapple Rag' by Scott Joplin

Movement practice

- (spaghetti)

   narrow body shape

   stiff jerky movements

   travelling in a straight pathway

   rolling or jumping

   flexible bendy body

   curling & turning pathway

- (jelly)

   solid strong movement

   fluid movement sliding & slithering shaking & trembling

- (bread dough)

   from small shape, stretching & collapsing, use space all around you

   sequence of extending & shrinking ending in firm, compact body shape

- (popcorn)

   explosive action from small body shape jumping, turning & travelling,

   springing & leaping in and out of others

Dance form

Individual dances sequencing 2 or 3 contrasting actions derived from one
food can be arranged in a number of ways. e.g. four groups may each
represent a different food and dance in sequence.

Note This dance could also relate to the science topic on change of state.

Theme – my home or homes and houses

● **Dance idea KS1 or 2: Doors In The House**

Learning objectives pattern and form in dance

Music 'In The Mood' by Glen Miller

Movement practice

- choose 2 or 3 actions to represent the activity in each room, make a motif
   for each action & form into a group dance

- bedroom, stretching, getting out of bed and dressing

   bathroom, shower, clean teeth & brush hair

   kitchen, make sandwich, stir cooking, wash pots etc.

- coach making the action clear in the space, develop the rhythm of the action,
plan the group formation, perform with the whole body

Dance form ABCD

Groups can each represent a room and perform in sequence with a whole
class ending for the dance.

● **Dance idea KS1 or 2: Behind the Washing Machine Door**

Learning objectives working with others or use of space

Music 'Spiral' by Vangelis

Movement practice

- moving freely in & out of others
- twisting & turning alone
- in a group of 5 or 6 move in & out of others, keeping close to others twisting and turning (tangled up), vary the levels
- travel as a group in a line, going in & out of other groups, twist & turn, making a curved pathway. Use different levels as you travel
- working alone travel freely – swerve all through the space
  leap, turn, travel
  leap, turn, descend & roll

Dance form ABABA or ABABC

A group interweaving, B group travelling C individual travelling twisting and turning.

● **Dance idea KS1 or KS2: The Castle Door**

The dance idea included earlier in the chapter in the section on dance and language may be appropriate to the theme of homes, door, or castles.

● **Dance idea KS2: In the attic**

Learning objective to communicate mood or character

Music silence, percussion or student composition

Properties a box of 'junk' from the attic, for example a shawl, an umbrella, a plastic flower, a child's fishing net, a newspaper, a piece of string, an envelope or letter.

Key questions What was the past of each item in the box? or what character used it? From these questions, the processes of Chapter 2 can help the children to find appropriate actions and forms for their group sequences.

Movement practices will obviously be specific to each stimulus. The common teaching points will be about body management, contrast in the structure and dynamics of the piece, management of transitions in the action to give fluid performance. (See Chapter 5, page 95, What does good movement look like?)

Dance form This idea could lead to a variety of solo, duo, trio and small group dances.

● **Dance idea KS1: My Toy Box**

Learning objective to express mood and feeling

Music 'Pizzicato Polka' from the *Simple Symphony* by Britten or from the 'Nutcracker Suite' by Tchaikovsky

Movement practice

- jack in the box

curling small and springing up

starting to bounce up slowly and then springing into a big body shape.

- marching soldier

  walking to a beat

  marching with knees high, marching in lines and patterns
- dancing doll

  head moves and looks round slowly

  arms and legs move stiffly

  whole body comes to life and dances freely in the space.
- robot, the same sequence as for the doll but the movement is jerky and the bodyshape angular throughout the dance.
- puppet, the same sequence can be adapted,

  stretch up and collapse down with your whole body

  head lifts, as if a string was pulling it.
- slinky spring

  curl and uncurl

  stretch and shrink

  travelling with a curved or circling pathway

  travel low and then roll

  sequence uncurling and curling travel to a new place, and repeat the dance
- top, observe a simple top and note the directions of the action and the speed variation

  turn and change levels, remember to practice to the right and left

  sway to build up momentum for the turn

  turn fast and jump

  turn fast and slow down

Dance form A B1 B2 B3 B4 A

Whole class dance, for example, the spring dance followed by groups of children representing each toy and a whole class ending.

● Dance idea KS 1 or 2: Building the House

Learning objective movement patterns from working actions or mechanical actions

Music from 'Appalachian Spring' or 'Rodeo' by Copland, or student composition

Movement practice

- preparing, patterns of movement from digging, pushing and pulling, building, carrying, sawing and laying bricks
- machines at work, slow strong movements and stiff jerking movements
- celebrating, folk dance steps to celebrate building the house

Dance form

KS 2 may be narrative: A preparing, B machines working, C building, D celebrating

Note This dance could be related to a theme of settlers making homes.

KS1 could use the story of the three little pigs as a stimulus for the dance form:

A skipping and dancing freely to represent the pigs playing at home
B looking for places and materials to build, walking and looking all around,
high and low,
C gathering materials and building with straw, sticks or bricks.
For this section the class can be in three groups and each can end by
encircling a member of the group to represent the animal in its home.

Theme – change

● Dance idea KS 1 or 2: Change of Form

Learning objective spatial understanding or working together as a group
Music music selected by the class, or percussion
Movement practice
- individually slowly growing into a shape and slowly changing shape
  slowly forming a shape and suddenly changing it
  shooting into a shape and slowly changing
- travelling and stopping in a shape
- as a group travelling as a line
  winding and unwinding a spiral
  forming a tangle from the line
- forming a group by jumping into the space in sequence 1, 2, 3, etc. Each
  child must look for a place to join the group shape or a space to fill
- as a group travel and stop in a group shape, repeat the phrase of movement
- as a group experiment with different formations

Dance form
KS1 A changing shape on the spot, B travelling, A repeat first section
KS2 the ABA form may be used as above or the group might select their own
form

Note Visual stimuli could be presented for this dance, for example, pictures of
rock formations, an elastic band, or a piece of string.

● Dance idea KS2: Volcanoes

Learning objective dynamic contrast in dance or working together
Music 'Uranus' from the *Planets Suite* by Holst
Movement practice
- individually growing into a shape
  travelling with turning twisting and rolling
  explosive jumps
- forming a group shape
  explosive jump from the shape
  travelling low and with twisting and turning
  forming a new shape, alone or with a new group

Dance form narrative: A eruption, B travelling like lava and C forming a shape
like solid lava.

Figures 3.5 and 3.6 *Forming a group shape contrasts with explosive jumping and travelling away from others. Children practise movements appropriate for a dance on the theme of volcanoes.*

Theme – growth

● Dance idea KS 1: Big and Small Dance

Learning objective spatial awareness or working with others

Music percussion

Movement practice

- alone – growing and shrinking, work on the floor and in the space, single body parts leading the stretching into the space, vary the speed of the actions.
- travel quickly, slowly, with increasing momentum, at different levels, combine travelling and jumping or travelling and rolling
- sequence growing lead by a single body part, extension of the whole body, travelling and shrinking
- work with a partner to make your dance together

Dance form narrative A grow, B travel and C shrink

● Dance idea KS 1: From Chrysalis to Butterfly

Learning objective strong and light movement or spatial awareness

Music percussion

Movement practice

- curling and uncurling, moving slowly and being still

repeat these actions working at floor level

pushing with different parts of the body, back, shoulder, knee etc.

- awareness of body parts, the arms moving successively, gently shaking and stretching
- travelling lightly in and out of others in the space
  work on use of the torso and feet to get a feeling of lightness in travelling
- death of the fly represented by stillness, shivering and falling

Dance form narrative: A escape, B extend, C travel, D end

Theme – minibeasts

● Dance idea KS 1: In the Compost Heap

Learning objective travelling or making motifs

Music children's percussion composition or selection from *Carnival of the Animals* by Saint Saens

Movement practice

- working on the floor, curling and uncurling, wriggling and rolling
- on feet, scuttle, dart, travel and stop in a small body shape
  travel in zig-zag pathways, and round in circles
- use arms and legs for spiky and jerking movements
  move as if you are carrying something heavy on your back
  move slowly as if you have just woken up
  move in and out of others

- sequence finding a body shape, curled, long or small, moving in that shape and then travelling

Dance Form narrative ABC

A children spaced randomly on the floor in stillness, B beginning to move at different times, C travelling in and out of others and ending in a large close group, like a heap.

Note Observation of creatures and their movement could provide the stimulus for this dance

Theme: light and colour

● Dance idea KS 2: In the Dark

Learning objective interpretation of stimulus, communication or forming the dance

Music The overture to *Cats* by Lloyd Webber or 'Dance Macabre' by Saint Saens

Process Use the questions suggested on page 47, allowing children to respond individually to the music before arriving at group dance ideas.

Movement practice will relate to the themes chosen but the music should guarantee some common practice particularly in the use of speed, strength and flow of movement.

Forming the dance The children may need help to establish the sections of the dance once they have improvised and developed a sense of the sequence.

● Dance idea KS1 or2: Reflections

Learning objective spatial awareness or working with others

Music 'Cavatina' by Myers or the theme from *The Piano* by Nyman

Movement practice work on pathways in space

- draw straight lines in the space, use space beside and above, as well as in front.

  vary the speed of the action, and the size

  make a sequence of 3 or 4 straight lines, have a clear start and known end, use contrast of time, size and levels

  perform your motif with the hand leading, the elbow, and then the shoulder

- draw curved pathways around the body, make a continuous line close to the body and away from it

  make a circular pattern in the space, develop this into a known sequence

- use this movement with a partner. Agree a starting place and then improvise to the music acting as a mirror and reflection. Form your dance from improvisation.

- KS 2 only: with a partner use the lesson material to form a motif to begin your dance

perform the motif at different levels, floor and standing
perform the motif with different body parts to lead the movement
use a turn or travelling to link two performances of the motif
work to perform your dance as a mirror and reflection

Dance Form If the dance is developed from improvisation, a clear start, middle section and known end is appropriate. Children structuring the duo may relate to the form of the music or decide on their own form.

● Dance idea KS1 or 2: Colour and Mood

Learning objective dynamic contrast or interpretation and communication through movement

Music could be suggested by the class

Process moods associated with colours will be agreed by the class and need not relate to the suggestions below

Movement practice

- red, anger: stamping, leaping and making strong gestures, like punching, travelling, leaping and turning with speed
- blue, peaceful: slow stretching and travelling, move lightly and gently
- grey, sad: slow, heavy movements
- yellow, lazy: stillness and slow movement, performing actions of work e.g. sweeping slowly

Dance form KS1 dance from improvisation for each mood.
KS2 children can make a solo from two contrasting moods

● Dance idea KS2: The Rainbow

Learning objective pathways and form in dance

Music theme from *The Onedin Line* by Khachaturian

Resources coloured ribbons or paper streamers can be used in the dance to create the shape of the rainbow in the air

Movement practice

- gesture making pathways in the space
  travelling freely and with step patterns
  travelling with leaping or with turning, use of different levels
- KS2 working as a group travel as a line, as a block, and as a wedge
- make a pattern of travelling as a line and then dancing together in a space. Each colour can be represented by a different group.

Dance Form A all groups stream across the space like a rainbow.
B two colour groups dance A all groups travel C three groups dance D whole class, circle or cross the space as a rainbow.

● Dance idea KS1 or 2: Me and My Shadow

Learning objective partner dance

Music 'Tiger Rag' by Scott Joplin

Movement practice
- awareness of individual body parts, nodding head, looking round with the head
  hands opening and closing fingers, arms making shapes and pathways in the air
- whole body stretches and makes bending shapes
- travelling and stopping suddenly
  walking, creeping, jumping and making patterns of steps
- with a partner follow my leader using slow and fast movement to catch your partner out
- decide on two or three different ways to travel in the dance

Dance form A travelling B dance of body shape and gesture A travelling

Theme – space or the planets

● Dance idea KS2: The Planets

Learning objective communication of mood or use of dynamic contrast

Music from *The Planets Suite* by Holst

Movement practice
- Mars: conflict, slow strong movements, strong fast actions, explosive jumping actions, group travelling to give a sense of power approaching, work on the crescendo and build up of power before explosion of action
- Venus: reconciliation, gentle rocking movements, slow light travelling, partner work, leading, following and surrounding a partner
- Mercury: travelling freely in the space with speed, groups can make individual step patterns
- Jupiter: travelling with simple step patterns create a group dance of celebration
- Saturn: slow heavy movements, faltering movements
- Uranus: rising up and down twisting and turning, building a crescendo before collapse

Note If the class focus on more than one planet ensure contrasting mood, for example, Mars and Venus or Mercury and Uranus

● Dance idea KS 1: Journey to a Strange Planet

Learning objective working together

Music 'Oxygene' (pt iv) by Jean-Michel Jarre

Movement practice
- weightlessness, slow light movement travelling with light slow steps, floating and turning in the space
- travelling and looking round using the head to lead the movement, feel the way with your feet, approach slowly and jump away, use different levels

- in groups of 3 or 5 slowly make a group shape, hold it and slowly move to form a new shape, practice and have a change of levels
- sudden jumping, spinning, then travelling freely in the space, to form a new group

Dance form Two-thirds of the class form the planet landscape by making group shapes which slowly change shape. A group explores the planet travelling in and out of the space and shapes and responding to the changes of shape. The group shapes explode and spin through space to reform. Each group can experience both roles and the dance could become a stimulus for story writing.

Theme – water

● Dance idea KS 1 or 2: Life under the Sea

Learning objective forming the dance or dynamic quality of movement
Music 'Sadko' by Rimsky-Korsakov
Movement practice derived from

- water or fish moving through the space: travelling with turning and changes of levels, flowing
- sea anemone: successive movement through the body and through the arms opening and closing
- crab: moving suddenly and stopping, scuttling, moving in different directions
- weed: swaying with the whole body and successive movement like a wave through the body

Dance form
KS1 allow children to make individual sequences relating to one creature and perform as a class dance
KS2 different creatures can be represented by different groups of children

● Dance idea KS 2: The Kraken

The same music might be used in response to Tennyson's poem The Kraken which might be introduced to older KS2 children.
Learning objective use of crescendo in the development of speed and energy of movement
Movement practice

- slowly awakening, uncurling individual body parts before getting onto the feet
- suddenly bursting, dashing, twisting and turning and leaping through the space
- falling, collapsing

Dance form A B C practise the three parts of the dance and work at the continuity and body management of transitions

● **Dance idea KS 1 or 2: A Day at the Sea Side**

Learning objective working with others or forming movement motifs

Music 'The Entertainer' by Scott Joplin

Movement practice

- KS1 travelling and carrying things
- KS2 travelling in small groups, think of group formation and then type of step
- swimming, action patterns or motifs for different strokes, vary the speed
- jumping over the waves, little jumps
- eating ice cream, make the action very big
- digging in the sand, look at different ways of digging
- building a sand castle
- running and jumping over the castle
- playing ball with a partner

Dance form A arrival at the sea side. B Individually or KS2 in groups, choose three or four actions to include in the dance. C decide on group or whole class ending for the dance.

Note Refer also to the work on Water in Chapter 4 (pages 82 and 83).
The movement words can be developed to movement tasks and practices.
Music 'Fingal's Cave' by Mendlessohn, or selection from 'Sea Interludes' from *Peter Grimes* by Britten.

● **Dance idea KS : Storms**

Learning objective developing variety of speed, flow and size of movements

Music 'Sea Interludes' by Britten from *Peter Grimes*

Movement practice

see unit of work in Chapter 4, pages 83 and 84

- work on the natural rhythm of the actions and the development of climax in the dance.

Theme – the seasons

● **Dance idea KS1: Autumn Dance – Conker Shells, Conkers and Leaves**

Learning objective body awareness or dynamic quality of movement

Music percussion

Movement practice

- spiky body shape and sudden straight movements on the spot and with jumping
- smooth round body shape and travelling slowly, rocking and rolling on the floor and travelling with turning at low level
- walking and kicking the leaves, stamping in the leaves, use different directions

travelling fast and slow like leaves being blown down
travelling with twisting and turning and different speeds
travelling and being still
Dance form sequence A stamping as if through the leaves, B the spiky and rolling
movements from the conker stimulus, C falling and tumbling into stillness

● Dance idea KS : Winter Snow and Ice

Learning objective understanding the dynamic quality of movement
Music percussion or theme from *The Snowman* by Blake
Movement practice see work on Snow in Chapter 2, page 37, and also tasks for
Snow Play on page 48 of this chapter

- making group shapes like snowflakes, one child travels and ends in a wide
  shape, 5 others join by touch and keep the wide symmetrical shape. The
  group shape can slowly move before slowly melting to the floor.

Dance form sequence the dance with contrast of dynamics, for example:
A Building a snowflake, travelling and being still
B gentle travelling like the snow falling
C slowly settling onto the floor
D spiky movements jagged like frozen forms
E stamping through the snow

● Dance idea KS : Spring

(See the suggestion under Growth on page 61.)

● Dance idea KS : Summer

(See the suggestion A day at the Seaside on page 66.)

Theme – place

● Dance idea KS1: In the Park

Learning objective spatial awareness
Music from 'St Paul's Suite' by Holst
Movement practice

- skipping freely in the space
  whole class circling and skipping in and out to the centre
- see suggestions from children's games unit of work in Chapter 4, page 84.

Dance form A skipping freely in the space, B dance alone from your favourite
game, C dance with a partner, D whole class circling and skipping to end the
dance.

● Dance idea KS1: At the Fair

Learning objective performing body actions or making dance motifs
Music fairground music
Movement practice

- Travelling with change of levels and making circular pathway, like a carousel
- patterns of movement from aiming at targets like coconuts
- spiralling down as if on a slide
- dodging in and out of others without crashing as if in dodgems

Dance form A in a circle whole class travel with rising and sinking, keeping in time. B individually choose a dance activity. C individually swerve in the space. A end as the dance began.

● Dance idea KS2: The USA

Learning objective forming a dance

Music from 'Rodeo', or 'Hoe Down', by Copland

Movement practice

- travelling and making step patterns to the music
- from individual steps decide on group step patterns
- find ways to turn, circle, in a star formation etc.
- decide on formations for the parts of dance

Dance form allow groups to form their own dances with three or four clear sections and steps.

Theme – place

For any country studied there is the possibility of arranging for a visiting dance group to perform at school (see Chapter 6, page 112). It is also possible to use the legend or mythology of the country's culture as a dance stimulus. The following dance outline can be adapted to a number of countries.

● Dance idea KS1: The Magic Carpet

Music appropriate to the country

Dance Form

A arrival and exploration of the environment, creeping & looking around

B playing or dancing with local children, simple dance patterns in circles or lines

C joining in traditional work, working actions

D final group dance using traditional music

Theme – history

Topics from history lend themselves to dances developed from everyday actions. To effectively translate the everyday action into dance children must be encouraged to:

- make a simple but clear action in the space

- make the action big and use their whole body to perform it
- develop the rhythm of the action

● Dance idea KS2: The Greek Olympic Games
Learning objective working with others or forming the dance
Music circle dance music and *Chariots of Fire* by Vangelis
Movement practice

- stretching preparation, make a rhythmic pattern
- javelin throw, travel and gesture
- discus swing, emphasise weight transfer, twist and jump
- jumping rhythm of swinging and jumping
- wrestling motif in pairs, weight transfer, swaying to dodging, twisting and turning
- running, slow motion running action and gesture of victory

Dance form narrative
A preparatory Greek style dance
B whole class dance stretching sequence
C groups dance their own event
D dance ends with runners crossing the room in victory

● Dance idea KS2: Viking raiders
Learning objective working with others or forming the dance
Music from 'Moldau' by Smetana and percussion
Movement practice

- building the boat, chopping, pulling, scraping, hammering and lifting
- sailing, pulling ropes and rowing
- exploring the land, creeping, looking, vary levels and speeds
- working actions in the village, sweeping, digging, grinding corn
- attack and conflict, creeping, running and leaping, partner work on attack and defend, work on weight transfer

Dance form
A preparation and journey
B life in the village
C arrival and attack

● Dance idea KS : Life in Medieval Castle or Preparing for a Tudor Feast
Learning objective working with others or forming the dance
Music from Early English Music or Renaissance music
Movement practice

- processional dance, slow stepping with upright posture
  patterns of stepping, for example, two steps forward and close feet together
dance the steps in circle and line patterns
- motifs from working actions, sweeping, stirring, grinding, chopping etc.

In groups choose two actions for your dance, have different formations the
two parts of your dance

Dance form A groups perform their dances from working actions to prepare
the feast. B class process into the hall and dance before the feast.

Note see 'Useful addresses, page 113, for the Dolmetsch Historical Dance
Society who may be able to help with resources.

● **Dance idea KS : Explorers and Discoverers: Life on a Sailing Ship**

Music from Jean-Michel Jarre or Vangelis

Movement practice

● stretching and waking up
● motifs from sweeping the deck, polishing the cannons, hauling up the sails,
  pulling, pushing the capstan
● exploring new land, creeping slowly with sudden turning, feeling the way,
  looking at different levels
● building fire and celebration dance

Dance form narrative sequenced as above

● **Dance idea KS 2: Victorian England**

● **Children's games** the unit of work Children's Games, Chapter 4, page 84,
  can be adapted to represent Victorian games.
● **The age of machines**

Music pupil composition

Movement practice

piston – moving backwards and forwards

shuttle – moving sideways

movements up and down

pendulum swinging

wheel circling

cog turning

in a group each perform one of your movements and give a sound
accompaniment to make a machine dance

● **The loom** – stimulus Van Gogh's picture 'The Loom', 1884 – can also lead
  to a group dance with a focus on the patterns of the warp and the weft. Use
  simple running steps make interweaving pathways like warp and weft, try
  half the class holding strips of paper like the warp and ask the others to
  dance between and under the strips

● **Dance idea KS 2: Britain at War The Bomb Attack**

Music 'The Dam Busters' March' or 'Knightsbridge March' by Coates

Movement practice

● motifs from actions of factory work, household work, or children playing,
  performed at normal speed and in slow motion
● sudden running and stillness in a group shape

- creeping out of the space and looking round, vary levels and timing of actions
- supporting, cradling and leading others

Dance form A in groups working dance

B stillness and rush to the group shape at the siren sound

C emerge and help others

D resume first dance but at slow speed

Theme – religious, social and moral education through dance

The dance suggested above might be regarded as an empathy exercise leading to a greater understanding of society and morality. For the children at the top of Key Stage 2 there are many issues which can be brought within their experience through dance.

● Dance idea KS : Isolation and Welcome

Learning objective working with others in trio

Music selected by group, for example, theme from *Schindler's List* by John Williams

Movement practice

- making simple spatial patterns or motifs derived from working together, perform as a duo and a solo
- change formation with a different person working alone before making a trio dance

Dance form AAB

● Dance idea KS : Conflict and Harmony

Movement practice

See notes under The Planets (Mars and Venus) on page 64.

● Dance idea KS1: Pollution or Litter

Learning objective basic actions performed with control

Music suggested by the class

Movement practice

- running in and out of others, travelling and turning
- lolly sticks, jumping and bouncing
- tin cans, spinning and rolling
- glass bottles, making jagged sharp shapes
- paper, skipping about in the space as if tossed around

Dance form A whole class travelling and turning like litter blown about.
B children choose their favourite action to represent litter. C conclusion travel into the centre to make a heap of litter.

- **Dance idea KS 2: Festivals**
- **Christmas** Originally carols were dances and children can make up simple steps and formations to dance their carols.
- **Chinese New Year** Use Chinese music and create a Dragon dance with the class following behind the dragon's head. The dancer with the head makes a winding pathway and swoops up and down through the space with the children watching carefully to follow (KS1)
- At **Hanukkah** introduce Israeli dance (KS2)

Theme – dance from art

- **Dance idea KS 2: Breugel Pictures of the Seasons**

Choose a picture and look at it together to suggest the actions which will form the motifs for a class dance. Each group can have two or three actions and sections in their dance and the whole class be brought together in a final celebration dance.

- **Dance idea KS 2: Textiles**
- different textiles may suggest different stories or characters as in a dance
- the texture of fabric can also lead to a movement sequence, for example, silk or chiffon suggest light floating movements, cotton may be strong and represented by pulling against a partner

- **Dance Idea KS 1 or 2: Colour Mixing**

Music instrumental music selected by the class
- each group can wear paper streamers of their group colour
- groups use simple travelling steps, skipping, polka and side step or gallop, to make a group dance with clear formation
- groups can move and create a new dance with another colour group.

Note The earlier dance idea on Colour and Mood, page 63, can also be considered in relation to art.

Theme – dance and music

The interpretation of music has already been discussed and throughout the text there are suggestions for music. Clear contrast within music can be helpful in developing more dramatic dance, for example 'The Gnome' from *Pictures at an Exhibition* by Mussorgsky.

Learning objective contrast in dance

Movement practice
- moving slowly and darting suddenly, strong heavy movement performed slowly and fast

- working at low and high levels
- individually improvise to the music using the vocabulary practised
- improvise as a group and then decide on the story of the dance

● Dance idea KS : Percussion

There have been suggestions for accompanying movement sequences with percussion. If instruments are limited it is possible to use the floor to drum or to use the body as an instrument. When introducing instruments it is wise to plan the session to ensure that you feel comfortable with the noise that will be generated.

● KS 1: Introducing percussion

Begin with the children sitting in a circle and listening to the instruments. Ask them to dance with their fingers according to the sounds and talk about the actions which suit each instrument. Ask the children to dance in the space responding to the same sounds and rhythms. Finally, sequence a set of sounds rhythmically to become the group dance.

● KS1 or 2: using percussion in small groups

Work on the movement practice, which might be a selection of actions, for example, jumping, turning and travelling. Allow each group a piece of percussion and ask children to take it in turns to accompany the actions that have been practised. Children might then progress to selecting two appropriate instruments to accompany their dance.

Developing response to rhythm and sound can become an exciting unit of work:

- ask the children to drum or to move and to repeat your rhythm or their partner's rhythm
- try completing a rhythmic phrase
- ask the children to each find a rhythm and then play their rhythm at the same time as their partner
- ask the children to have a conversation without words but by drumming in the floor or an instrument.

Develop these ideas and ask the class to have a conversation with actions and vocal sounds but not words.

The dance ideas in this chapter can all be used in conjunction with the core and foundation subjects of the 1995 National Curriculum. The chapter has related dance ideas to the current structures of the curriculum documents. Mindful of change in education it is important to emphasise that the material is of itself valid and has a contribution to make to the education of the child.

Planning, progression and development

Having begun to teach dance in the school, there is a need to consider the progression of work through the primary years. This chapter is concerned with short, medium and long term planning. It invites reflection on the expectations of work and achievement at different stages in the primary school.

TEACHER APPROACHES TO PLANNING

This book is concerned with the process of becoming a dance teacher. For teachers new to dance the first question may be, Can I deliver a sequence of lessons? or even a lesson? For this reason the chapter deals with medium and short-term planning before addressing whole school plans. The medium- and short-term planning is concerned with sequences of lessons, or units of work, and lessons The National Curriculum emphasises long-term planning through its reference to achievement within Key Stages, and assessment against the End of Key Stage Descriptions.

Within school, planning can be described as a top down process; from school whole curriculum plan, to subject plan for the school, to Key Stage plan, to year plan, to unit of work plan and finally to the lesson plan. By contrast teaching may be regarded as a bottom up process the experience being developmental from the lesson, to the sequence of lessons or unit of work, and the school subject plan. Central to both processes are the child, continuity and progression of content.

For teachers of dance and Physical Education, the immediate daily concern is the class and the development of the pupils. Fostering development means placing the lessons taught in the context of the child's whole school career. For any class there is a need to plan with reference to previous experience, present abilities and with an awareness of future expectations.

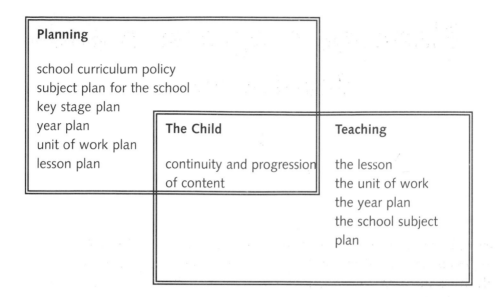

Planning

school curriculum policy
subject plan for the school
key stage plan
year plan
unit of work plan
lesson plan

The Child

continuity and progression
of content

Teaching

the lesson
the unit of work
the year plan
the school subject
plan

When talking about planning it is also important to consider the experience of the teachers. There is a need to recognise varied attitudes, aptitudes and levels of confidence within the staff delivering dance in school.

Three broad developmental phases of becoming a teacher of dance are:

- initial
- emergent and
- established teacher.

Each raises different planning questions and concerns. With progression through these phases comes a shift of focus from the teacher to the learner.

In the initial phase the concerns may be teacher centred relating to issues of content and delivery;

- issues of content, such as having something to teach, getting ideas for dances and having enough material for the whole lesson
- issues of delivery may involve knowing what to ask of the children and how to set clear tasks to which the children can respond
- issues of organisation and management of dance lessons have much in common with all Physical Education lessons and may relate to,the children as a class, groups or individuals, to resources and equipment or to time within the lesson. Safety and maintenance of control within the lesson will be a prime consideration within the planning.

The emergent dance teacher has begun to solve the challenges of content and the focus moves to the quality of teaching and learning taking place. The reflective teacher observes and evaluates the work. This leads to new questions:

- How will the children gain greater knowledge, movement skill or understanding of the dance activity as a result of the lesson or the sequence of lesson?
- Exactly what will be gained or learned?
- How will I know if there is learning?
- How can I extend these children?

The established teacher is better able to consider the lesson or unit of work in the context of the child's past and future experience of the subject and may be increasingly concerned with issues of:

- improving the quality of bodily performance and choreographic ability
- differentiation in teaching to meet the needs of the whole class
- ownership of the lesson and the dance. This prompts questions about who plans the dance and how the teacher shares planning and ownership.

The experienced teacher may consider the development of a range of teaching styles which increase the learners' contribution to, and control of, the lessons.

Suggestion Reflect on the three stages of becoming a dance teacher and identify your present abilities.

PLANNING FOR TEACHING AND LEARNING, EVALUATION AND ASSESSMENT

Teaching and learning objectives

Effective dance teaching requires that each lesson or series of lessons has a clear objective. It is important that this is shared with the children, not only so that they know what we are hoping to achieve but also, so that we, as teachers, make a clear statement of expectation to our pupils.

The objective is a statement of the learning we hope to facilitate through the lesson or sequence of lessons. In dance as in other curriculum areas learning is a complex process.

Objectives may relate to:

- the movement knowledge and the children's movement vocabulary

- the forming of dance
- the performance of the dance
- the development of skills of evaluation and appreciation
- working in relationship to others.

They may be expressed in the terms of the National Curriculum End of Key Stage Descriptions for Key Stages 1 and 2 which reflect the processes implicit in the attainment target:

- planning and performing
- linking actions together
- improving the performance
- working with others
- making judgements about performance

When planning a unit of work with several lessons it is important that there are not too many learning objectives. The children may engage in a variety of movements or dance-making skills but the teacher and the children need a clear and limited learning focus of one or two objectives. The learning objectives should answer the questions:

- What things will the child be able to do, know or understand at the end of the unit of work as a result of the lessons?
- How will the movement vocabulary be extended and what new knowledge or understanding of dance will be gained?

Planning with assessment and evaluation in mind

When planning a lesson a planning check may ensure that the PE attainment target is being met. Ask yourself the question;

Where in the lesson can the child plan, perform and evaluate?

It is important to plan opportunities for the children to practise the skill of evaluation.

For each lesson or sequence of lessons identify how you will know if the learning objective has been achieved. What will be the evidence of learning or skill achieved? or what are the teacher's assessment criteria?

RECORDING SHORT- AND MEDIUM-TERM PLANNING

There is no single correct way to record planning but the recorded plan is a teaching tool and the process of recording can be a valuable part of the preparation.

The short-term or lesson plan might include:

- a statement of learning objectives

- a statement of the evidence of learning. What activity or behaviour will show that the objectives are met? Alternatively this may be written as a statement of assessment criteria to help in the formative assessment during and at the end of the lesson.

- the actual movement action tasks to be set in the lesson. Each lesson may have three or four main tasks which can be extended and presented to give repeated movement experience.

- a note of your own role in response to the children's activity. What will you expect to see as you scan the room, what quality of movement will you look for? What might you need to coach or remind children of as they work?

- a note on the organisation of resources

- a planning check might identify the lesson tasks which enable the children to meet the process of the attainment target. Where in the lesson can the children plan, perform and evaluate their work?

Medium-term planning involves developing a unit of work or sequence of lessons

- The sequence of lessons should be coherent and have a logical development.

- Each lesson should have clear movement vocabulary or skill development content.

- Tasks to develop other learning should be clear, for example, if the objective is to develop a dance with a partner there may be a note of strategies to help children plan together.

- The unit plan should identify the three or four main movement tasks of the teaching for each lesson, the lesson plan will detail the extension of each task.

Table 4.1 *Lesson plan KS 1 – pathways on the floor*

POS: Dance	Year group: KS 1, Yr 1/2
Unit: space & form in dance	Resources: percussion music – folk dance – reel
Movement objective: to establish awareness of floor pathways – curved, straight	**Evidence of learning**: children will be able to perform & through observation identify curved & straight pathways
Other learning objective: revision of travelling – skipping, gallop/side step	**Evidence of learning**: children will perform travelling actions with quality
Movement task	Observation, resources, organisation
Introduction, warm-up • whole body 'wake up' • draw circles with face, shoulders, hips, knees • strech full body & shake down to the ground	– NB face circles vertically *not* tipping head back – safety point – percussion

Development 1:
 • skipping – freely in space skipping high – to elevate
 • draw curved pathway in air repeat task – use other arm & all space
 • skip curved pathway
 	
 • partner work – A stands still & observes
      B skips in & out of other standing still repeat task
      B observes
      A skips
 • gallop – side step in the space
 • gallop in straight line on floor
 • partner work – A stands still & observes
      B gallops in straight lines in & out of other standing still repeat task
      B observes
      A gallops
 • introduce music & listen – sitting skip then gallop to sound
	– observe – use of space, can they skip?, note toes, knees & elbows elbows & knees high
	 – look at examples – NB good starting position – lean into your position with whole body
	 – coach space above, beside, in front etc. – in & out of others
	 – observation/feedback points – does your partner make a curved line?
	
	 – observe use of space & correct stop
	 – coach stop & turn – observation/ feedback points
	
	 – music

Development 2 • partner dance – decide skip curved pathway – gallop straight travel to meet your partner practise, observe two pairs • find way to turn with partner decide how to travel with your partner skip curved pathway – gallop straight • perform – travel to partner – turn – travel with partner • decide formation for travelling at end • practise dance • if time view groups/half class **Conclusion and cool down** slowly draw circles, lines & shapes with named body parts – relaxation	– music – space out – across room from partner – class feedback on pathways – observe & try ways shown – observe pathways

PE unit of work		Date:	
POS: Dance	Key Stage: 1	Year: 1/2	
Title: Space & Form			
Movement objective	experience curved and straight pathways		
Evidence of learning:	the child can travel in curved and straight pathways		
Other learning objective:	to create and recall pathways in a simple dance		
Evidence of learning:	the child can create and recall a dance with simple pathways		
Dance stimulus:	leading towards folk dance		

Movement content	Resources

1   Skip curved pathway
   – gallop straight pathway
   – choose skip curves/gallop straight travel to partner
   – find ways of turning with partner
   – choose way to travel with partner, as above
	country dance music
	tambour
	introduce music
	music

2   Revise dance so far
   – travel as pair to four skip curves or gallop straight
   – turn as a 4, find ways & practice
   – practise travelling in line of 4
   – perform dance so far
	music
	
	maybe tambour here
	music

3   Revise dance
   – work on circling & travelling as 4 walk & skip
   – try whole class ending into 1 line/circle
   – perform dance
	
	tambour
	music

4   Perform advance as made
   – work on whole class patterns of walking
      e.g. spirals, archways, circle, in & out from centre & round to right & left
   – add whole class ending to the dance
	music
	tambour

5   Begin new dance from visual stimulus
   – trace pattern in the air
   – experience pattern by walking, running, jumping it
   – dance your pattern
   – choose 2 friends and look at the dances
      Are they like the patterns?
	set of 5/6 visual patterns spirals, zig-zag etc.
	
	music – Scott Joplin rag

6   Continue above idea, work in pairs
   – partner A make a dance from a straight line pattern, B from a curved pattern
   – review and practise to improve
   – combine 2 patterns to make a dance with 2 motifs
	music as above

Table 4.2 *Unit plan KS 1 – developing form in dance*

How many lessons should I spend on a dance? This is a question teachers have often asked. There is no simple answer. At Key Stage 1 a single lesson may give a complete dance experience, some dances may take two or three lessons and some become much longer projects. The length of time spent on a dance must be determined by the engagement of the class. A unit of work may involve several dances as the examples show. A unit plan is only a plan and should be flexible, for example lessons three and four of the unit above might be adjusted according to the responses of the class.

There are varied learning outcomes possible from a single dance experience and the teacher must select the learning focus from the possibilities presented by a single dance idea. In the Key Stage 1 unit on space and form in dance, the general learning objective might well have been concerned with awareness of others in the environment (General Requirements 2d). This unit requires individual and negotiated decision making as well as sensitivity to others moving as a group in the whole working space.

PE unit of work		Date:
POS: Dance	Key Stage: 2	Year: 4/5
Unit Title: Developing form in dance		
Movement objective: to experience and create step patterns with clear group formations		
Evidence of learning: children will create step patterns and line dances		
Other learning objective: understanding form in dance, e.g. A B C B D B (a simple chorus dance)		
Evidence of learning: the children will be able to identify the form of their dance		
Resources: circle dance music, 'Maple Leaf Rag' by Scott Joplin		
Movement objective		Resources
week 1 – warm-up, rhythmic games – teach step patterns: step step close,step step stamp, – children invent step patterns – in groups, look at friend's patterns – all learn 1 step and perform in a line learn a second step and perform in a circle		tambour introduce music, circle dance music, greetings dance
week 2 – warm-up, rhythmic patterns – revise dance with A and B patterns – add 2 new steps C & D to dance in line formation dance form A B C B D B, with b in circle formation – look at possible formations – choose and practise dance formations in groups – perform dances		music as above

week 3 – dance from a visual pattern
– revise travelling
– choose pattern to walk, run jump etc.
– choose 3 ways to travel your pathway skip, walk & jump
  work on contrast; levels, speeds, energy or flow of
  movement (form ABC)
– observe partners sequence & provide sound
		
		percussion

week 4 – pair dance with directions
– warm-up music as last week revise directions in travelling
– choose 3 ways to travel or 3 steps & practise
  choose 3 directions and relate them to your three steps
  e.g. skip forwards, jump sideways and walk back
– develop pattern and work on contrast; use of levels, timing
– show a partner and learn one of the dance sequences
	'Maple Leaf Rag'

week 5 – warm up as last week. – revise and perform dance made last week – revise formation possibilities & decide on formation – add second sequence to the dance and vary the formation – create ending and identify form A B A, or A B C etc.	music as above

Table 4.3 *Unit plan KS 2 – developing form in dance*

This unit is also planned with several short dances offering different experiences of forming a dance. It might be that any of the dances would be extended to take more time. At the end of the unit it is valuable to perform and review all of the dances made. This allows opportunity to enjoy known dances, and to value the work done.

The above units are both concerned with spatial knowledge and elements of dance form. They are in part derived from dance stimulus in the form of folk dance music.

The process model introduced in Chapter 2 may also be developed into units of work. An example from the stimulus of water follows.

Title: Water

Stimulus	Action			Accompaniment
flowing	travelling	curve pathway	flowing continuous	shake tambourine
drip	drop (head/arm action)		sudden staccato	tap tambourine
rushing	travelling		vary speed and momentum	shake and vary speed/volume
swirling	travel and descend	spiral pathway change levels		
roar	travel	vary levels	vary energy (surge)	
lap	sway (hand gesture or whole body)		slow but constant speed light	cymbal

Stimulus	Action		Accompaniment	
swell	sway and vary levels		slow and light vary speed	
crash	impact: hands beat/ rebound people rebound	vary levels	strong	
	travel impact rebound and recover		sense of crescendo	drum
bubbling	jumpy		light and fast	finger tap on tambour

Table 4.4 *Process chart – identifying the content of the lesson*

PE unit of work			Date:	
POS: Dance		**Key Stage:** 2	**Year:**	
Unit Title: Dynamics/quality of movement in dance				
Movement objective: To perform actions with contrast and control of quality, particularly varied speed and momentum/flow				
Evidence of learning: Pupils will be able to travel and dance at varied speeds, and with varied momentum whilst maintaining control and good body awareness				
Other learning objective: To compose alone and with others				
Evidence of learning will be seen in the structure and performance of the *known and repeated* individual, and group dance and in the partner dance				
Dance stimulus: Water **Music**: 'Sea Interludes' by Britten and 'Singing in the Rain' by Freed				

Movement objective	Resources, Grouping, Observation points
week 1 – travelling [flowing], spiral [swirling] travel with momentum – [gushing] – sway[swell & lap] – individual sequence from the words lap, flow, swirl or gush. i.e. sway, travel, spiral or vary flow of travel – practise and perform personal sequence	introduce music
week 2 – recall and revise dance from week 1 – fast light travelling and jumping [bubbling] – crashing, impact of hands meeting and falling away, impact and rebound, as if waves crashing together – incorporate one new movement, motif into your dance – perform and review in pairs/groups.	

week 3 – in groups perform dance to date, discuss group endings – in groups, linear travel [streaming] and represent wave breaking, e.g. travel forward with lift, turn and recede low – in groups decide on one activity/motif to add and an ending for the dance – review group dances to date	? possibly use paper streamers in blue/green colours
week 4 – practise dances with emphasis on motor performance; balance, control, awareness of whole body – perform dances and evaluate dance & performance	? video work
week 5 pair dance, stimulus 'Singing in the Rain' – step patterns, walking and jumping, missing the puddles – vary weight, step lightly and stamping – from individual patterns & motifs make dance with partner – view and perform	'Singing in the Rain'
week 6 – perform and review pair dance – perormance of both dances in the unit of work	invite audience from year group
Planning check: What will the children know, understand or be able to do as result of this unit of work?	

Table 4.5 *Unit of work KS 2 – developing speed, tension and continuity of movement*

Mimetic action, movement patterns derived from mime, can also be used in creating dance. The following unit may relate to a topic on children.

PE unit of work		Date:
POS: Dance	**Key Stage:** 2	**Year:**
Unit Title: Forming group dance		
Movement objective: to develop skills of making motif and group formation		
Evidence of learning: children will create individual motifs and group formation		
Other learning objective: development of interpersonal skills and sensitivity to others		
Evidence of learning: children will be able to negotiate group decisions and be responsive to others in improvisation		
Stimulus: topic Children's Games or Victorian Children's Games		
Movement objective		**Resources**
week 1 warm up revise ways of travelling – develop motifs from hide & seek, hopscotch, & ball games, throw/catch, kick and bounce – individually select 3 to form your own dance music, have contrast of travelling and on the spot motifs – practise and perform		tambour to emphasise rhythm
week 2 warm up as last week – introduce/develop new motifs, skipping, skipping and clapping rhymes – revise individual dance		tambour music

– add pair dance, agree game activity and improvise; do not organise but develop the dance from improvising – perform both parts of the dance	
week 3 warm up include work on feet – revise and refine dance so far – groups of 4 or 6 and decide on a game activity, individually create motif, look at motifs in the group and agree one to learn – agree formation line or circle – repeat group process with new game and include new formation. This time can you travel as a group? – demonstrate group formation and travelling possibilities	neat travelling
week 4 warm up as last week – refine and perform dance so far – create ending, probably group circling pattern	
week 5 invite another class to see the final performance	

Table 4.6 *Unit of work KS 2 – forming a group dance*

PROGRESSION AND DEVELOPMENT IN DANCE

Teachers must be concerned with progression and development of dance within the Key Stage and within the school. As with planning units of work there is no single way to chart progression but there are many dimensions of development to be considered:

- establishing the concept of a dance
- establishing the concept of form in dance
- understanding the use of motif in dance
- development of the use of dynamic quality of movement
- improved understanding and use of space
- ownership of the dance by the pupils.

Progression depends on our supporting the children through the task setting and also upon holding expectations of their development. The following statements of expectation demonstrate progression through the school.

Progression in the concept of a dance and form in dance

Key Stage 1:

- 'my/our dance', the teacher uses language to establish the concept of dance
- the dance starts and ends clearly, although this may be teacher-controlled

- awareness of 'We start like this . . ., then we do . . ., and then we end like this'.

Key Stage 2:

- awareness of content, sequence and form (pattern)
- awareness of contrast within the dance.

A sense of motif and motif development is possible at the end of this stage, but this will only emerge if we have taught that movement pattern becomes a motif and if we ask children to create and develop these motifs within the dance.

Development of a motif

A motif is a movement pattern which is composed and remembered by the dancer. Motifs can be drawn from action words: travel, tip and turn or stretch, travel and drop. Motifs can also be drawn from an everyday action, but it must become emphasised. The action of throwing and catching a ball can become stretch, travel and drop.

Motifs can be varied in many ways, for example:

- they can be performed at a different level
- one part of the motif can be repeated
- the phrase can be performed at a different speed.

Progression in body action and awareness

Key Stage 1:

- mastery of basic ways of travelling: walk, skip, gallop, and of some whole body actions, for example turn or stretch
- the ability to link two or three actions into a sequence
- the ability to work with control and manage weight transfer

Key Stage 2:

- increased awareness of extremities and whole in harmony, i.e. better awareness of the centre of the body
- good management of body, balance and control at all times
- good body management and control in transition from one movement to another.

Figures 4.1 and 4.2 *Progression in the use of contrasting speed in movement. Older Key Stage 2 children are able to approach slowly and suddenly turn away attending to the time and spatial aspects of the movement. [Figure 4.1] This is a progression from the simpler action task of creep and jump away from your partner. [Figure 4.2]*

Progression in spatial learning

Key Stage 1:

Teach and use pathways on the floor and in the air:

- levels
- directions

Key Stage 2:

- revise all of the above knowledge and expect children to use it individually and in group situations
- work on symmetry and asymmetry within the body and within a group of dancers
- spatial patterns and formations in groups

Progression in use of dynamics

Key Stage 1:

Experience of fast /slow, strong/light, controlled /flowing.

Key Stage 2:

- master two or three qualities in combination, for example, fast and flowing and light or strong movement
- show better control of dynamics and be able to vary the quality within a dance if appropriate.

Progression in the ownership of the dance

- the dance making may be teacher led, with children making some decisions, for example they may suggest how the dance ends
- the teacher may frame or structure the dance but the children make their own movement patterns or motifs
- the children decide the scenario and take more responsibility for deciding the actions and qualities they need to work on for their dance. The teacher works on movement training and helping the children to form the group dance.

This is a progression which happens across the Key Stages according to the teacher and the children. It is not an age-related progression although age and experience are both relevant.

Figure 4.3 and 4.4 *Key stage 1 work towards English Folk dance as they make patterns of travelling in lines and circles. Travelling together requires awareness of others and co operation.*

Figure 4.5 *Older children developing a trio work together with sensitivity.*

WHOLE SCHOOL PLANNING

Just as the whole PE programme is planned with a balance of different experiences, so the dance programme deserves to be carefully structured. There are different ways in which this might be approached.

Key Stage 1 teachers have responsibility for establishing the foundations of the movement vocabulary and so it may be appropriate to express the plan in those terms.

Assuming three PE sessions a week and units lasting half a term, you might include four units of dance work in the six units of Physical Education taught each year at Key Stage 1. Each unit can have a different movement focus:

- body awareness
- spatial awareness
- dynamics of movement
- a unit leading into country/cultural dance.

Key Stage 1 dance plans

● Reception

1 self in space and response to percussion, moving and stopping

2 travelling and use of pathways

3 body awareness, big and small body shapes and movements

4 vocabulary of body actions travel, turn, jump, extend and contract.

● Year 1

1 body awareness

2 dynamics – quick slow/light heavy

3 dance using spatial themes – pathways and levels. This could lead to English country dance style work.

4 introduce pair work, i.e. observing and talking to partner about their work.

Year 2

1 Body actions, with a focus on improving performance or linking body actions

2 dynamics stressed, combining qualities, for example strong and slow, fast and strong

3 dance using spatial themes, directions and patterns of stopping and jumping, partner and group work is possible

4 simple country dance introduced.

Key Stage 2 dance plans

Key Stage 2 may also offer thee sessions a week and have three units of dance in the year. In some situations where there are fewer and longer lessons, there may only be two units of dance. The two planning outlines following express the unit objectives in terms of the End of Key Stage Description.

● KS 2: Planning against the EKSD with two units a year

Teachers can identify specific learning objectives and criteria for assessment relating to the selected statements; for example in year 6 children should be able to create warm up sessions appropriate to dance and/or perform with stamina throughout the lesson.

year 3	performance – link actions	dance-making – plan dance
year 4	performance – improve	make judgements – evaluate performance
year 5	performance – work with others	dance-making – plan and perform
year 6	performance – health related	make judgements – evaluate

● KS 2: Planning against the EKSD with three units a year

Specific unit objectives can be formed relating to each statement.

year 3	plan & perform – structure dance	link actions	make judgements
year 4	improve performance – body awareness transitions in dance	work with others	make judgements
year 5	plan & perform – motif developments	health focus in warm up & cool down, stretching & flexibility in body preparation	make judgements
year 6	improve and perform dynamic contrast	work with others	make judgements

Dance does need to be taught throughout the PE programme if there is to be good development of body control, movement vocabulary, dance-making and dance-appreciation skills. It is also important that there is variety of focus in the progression of units of dance, but also that the different aspects of the EKSD are represented. There is certainly more to dance than 'doing something to fit in with the topic.'

Appreciating, evaluating and assessing dance

This chapter examines the nature of the processes before focusing on promoting children's evaluation of dance, and the assessment and the reporting requirement facing the teacher.

The generalist teacher within primary education faces two challenges: firstly, enabling the children to evaluate in order to meet the Physical Education attainment target, and secondly, to meet the requirement to report on children's performance and learning in Physical Education. In order to do this there is a need to assess children's knowledge, understanding and physical achievement, considering these in relation to the appropriate End of Key Stage descriptor in the National Curriculum for Physical Education. Meeting the statutory requirement is essential but it is also important to consider the intrinsic value of the processes we engage in.

Before the development of the National Curriculum, dance teaching had an established strand of appreciation. Traditions of critical appreciation exist in relation to all other art forms and also feature in the curricula of literature, music and the visual arts. Whilst appreciation, evaluation and assessment all have a common critical element, there are also differences between the processes:

● Appreciation involves a degree of analysis, critical evaluation, and can also become a tool of education about dance. Dance analysis and appreciation has become a sub-discipline within the academic study of dance. The term 'appreciation' is frequently used when referring to the work of an established artist, either a choreographer or performer. The basic processes of appreciation and evaluation are similar.

- Evaluation involves looking, considering and making a judgement about the process or product. Perhaps this word suggests a more immediate involvement with the work as creator or performer. This is also the language of the Physical Education attainment target.

- Assessment, whilst it also involves making critical judgement, has an added dimension of measurement. In the context of primary Physical Education teachers will assess achievement or attainment against the criteria of the End of Key Stage Description.

All forms of appreciation, evaluation and assessment demand the identification of criteria by which judgements are made. When looking at dance the criteria may address:

- the performance of the piece (Programme of Study 3a both Key Stages)
- the structure and form of the work (Programme of Study 3b)
- communication or transmission of meaning (Programme of Study study 3c)

These three elements of the dance can all be related to the National Curriculum programme of study.

The nature of dance has given rise to concerns about exactly what is being assessed. Teachers have also identified the difficulty of looking at a class and seeing what everyone is doing.

The prerequisites skills of assessment are:

- knowing what to look for
- observing, and
- managing the observation.

EVALUATION AND ASSESSMENT WITHIN THE LESSON

Teachers have long recognised that formative assessment is an essential of good practice. To assess the children's responses during the lesson enables the teacher to appropriately plan the next phase of the session or the next lesson in the sequence. As a part of the teaching process, formative assessment involves observing, giving feedback and talking to children about their work. Assessment of the responses and performance of the class also facilitates the evaluation of the teaching which has taken place and the learning which may have occurred.

Within the lesson observation of performance may focus on:

- movement vocabulary
- motor control
- achievement of a particular skill
- quality of movement or control of dynamics
- managing transitions from one movement to another
- creation, performance or recall of a sequence or dance
- good use of the space
- awareness and sensitivity to others

What does good movement look like?

The following questions may help to focus the observation:

- Is there control of the body?
- Is there good extension of the body, stretched fingers and toes?
- Is the whole body involved in the movement?
  Is the centre/trunk involved or does the child move and wave the arms?
  Does the head follow the line of the spine?
  Does the movement flow through the body?
- Is there good management of body weight?
  Is there balance and control in stillness?
  Is there smooth weight transfer in travelling?
- Does the child use a wide base for stability?
- Is there good transition from one movement to another? Does the action flow?

What does good dance look like?

Children, particularly in the later stages of Key Stage 2, will also benefit from feedback on their performance as dance makers. This requires observation and evaluation against criteria related to the structure of dances:

- Is there good use of contrast? contrast in dynamics, levels, size of movements, movement and stillness etc.
- Does the dance have a form, a known beginning , middle and end?
- Do the children perform with total bodily commitment, are they fully engaged in the movement?

Simpler criteria for the end of Key Stage 1 are:

Figures 5.1, 5.2 and 5.3 *What does good movement look like? Look at the three pictures and consider the quality of body awareness and control in relation to the question on page 95. Watching others helps children to develop awareness of movement quality. [Figure 5.3]*

- Is there variety in the dance?
- Does the dance have a clear start and a clear ending?

Both of these sets of questions can be effectively shared with children. The questions on movement might also be used with a photographic display in the hall. This will help children to develop the skills of looking and making critical judgements about Physical Education.

Helping children evaluate

When we help children to evaluate work we also develop their observation skills and their ability to think and talk about movement and the form or performance of the dance. Opportunities for making judgements and evaluating must be built into the lesson.

Figures 5.4 and 5.5 *Contrast on levels and body shape add interest to a duo.*

Questions to promote self assessment are part of ongoing teaching. For example,

Do you change levels in your dance? or
Think about your dance which part do you most need to practise?

Paired work or reciprocal teaching can be a helpful strategy to develop pupil evaluation skills. When one partner observes, the other also has more space in which to work and with older children working in a small space this can allow improved quality of performance.

The following questions may help to focus the children's evaluation:

- Did your partner meet the task? For exmaple, did he/she make a sequence of three movements?
- Can you tell your partner something you liked about their dance?
- Can you tell your partner which part of their dance was best and explain why you thought it was good?
- Which part of the dance should your partner work on to improve it?
- How can your partner make the movement look better?
- How can your partner make his/her body look better as he/she dances?

Most of these questions can be asked of the Key Stage 1 child. It does take time to establish the practice of looking at your partner, but children of this age group are able to identify simple task completion and talk about their partner's work.

At Key Stage 2 the process of evaluating a friend's work can help children to focus on the quality of their own actions. Peer assessment will also take place as groups perform their 'work in progress' or their actual dances. The process of showing work provides the opportunity for performance as well as developing the skill of making judgement.Initially the criteria for looking may be open, for example:

I would like you to watch and then say what you like about the dance.

With practice, the Key Stage 2 class can be asked to focus on specific aspects, such as body management or the dance structure.

The processes of the teacher's formative assessment and the children's ability to evaluate are complementary. You may consider the use of video recording to help you in this process. To record work in progress and completed dances can help develop the children's skills of appreciation and evaluation.

At the end of a unit of work or at the end of the key stage, summative assessment may be made noting the achievements of individual children.

Developing appreciation of dance may be helped by the use of videotaped dance. Children and teachers can look at a performance against criteria of performance, or they may look for the movement motif, or the structure of the dance.

DIAGNOSTIC ASSESSMENT

Much attention is given to the current requirements of the National Curriculum but the need for reporting should not dominate our thoughts about assessment. Looking and making judgements about the children we teach is an essential part of the teaching process. There may be some children for whom we need to make a more diagnostic observation. The pupil with motor difficulty or delayed motoric development may become obvious in Physical Education. If a child is not achieving 'normal' performance in Physical Education, is constantly noticed for lack of co-ordination or failure to achieve fundamental motor skills, it may be helpful to ask a classroom assistant to carry out a special observation.

You may look at aspects of the pupil's performance such as:

- does the child follow basic instructions, for example move and stop?
- motor control
- control of stopping – good/poor
- balance in basic actions – good/poor
- jumping – does the child push up or just drop down?
- control and use of appropriate strength of action, is there tension making actions jerky?
- spatial awareness
- awareness of self in relation to others in the space – good/poor
- directional awareness, left/right – good/poor
- time engaged on task – note time not on task for a period of the lesson
- look at the use of particular body parts: hands, feet, knees, eyes etc.

Simple observations and statements can be discussed with the SEN Co-ordinator and support staff. They may also contribute to report for other specialists who work with the child. Full diagnostic assessment is a complex and skilled task carried out over a period of time, but detailed observation can answer the question 'What is really going on?' and give a greater knowledge of the individual child. Reference to the developmental stages of basic activities may help teachers identify delayed development. (Gallahue 1996) Class teachers may be able identify the movement problems and skills requiring extra practice. They may also be able to contribute physical activities to the learning plan for children.

ASSESSMENT OF ATTAINMENT IN RELATION TO END OF KEY STAGE DESCRIPTIONS (EKSD)

This represents an important dimension of assessment within the National Curriculum. It is important to identify a limited aspect of any EKSD to assess at any one time, i.e. through any lesson or unit there should be a limited but clear focus on what is being taught and therefore assessed. The EKSDs can form the criteria for the child's performance in dance.

● Key stage 1

- Plan and perform simple skills. The child can travel safely in a space in several ways, for example, stepping, skipping, galloping.

- Show control in linking actions together, for example, running and leaping, travelling and turning.

- Improve performance through practising. This implies that the child is developing movement memory and can repeat an action phrase.

- Work alone – respond to task set by the teacher. Not all children can do this, occasionally a pupil will have to look and rely on others for ways to respond.

- Work with a partner – the children can copy a partner, lead a partner, or perform a simple dance with a partner

- Talk about what they and others have done. This may be telling the story of the dance or it could be looking and talking abut how a particular activity is performed, for example, talking about the body shape or the use of the legs and feet.

- Make simple judgements. For example, the children can see if a partner has achieved a simple task, such as travelling in two different ways. Older Key Stage 1 children are able to make evaluative statements and identify such things as good use of the body.

- Talk about the changes that happen to their bodies during exercise. Key Stage 1 children should be able to make simple statements about breathing, heartbeat etc.

● Key Stage 2

- Find solutions to challenges., This may be in terms of physical challenge to achieve good execution of a movement or action phrase.

- Respond imaginatively to tasks. A child may respond imaginatively to a stimulus presented, being able to suggest ideas for a dance. Alternatively you may see a child responding to a movement task in a particularly interesting or imaginative way.

- Practise, improve and refine performance, both the individual movement phrase and the whole dance performance.
- Repeat movements with increased control and accuracy.
- Work alone.
- Work in pairs. Working with a partner and others has the dimension of awareness of the other in performance as well as the ability to share the development of a dance idea.
- Work in groups. Through Key Stage 2 it is reasonable to expect increasing independence in the ability to work together and make dance.
- Make judgements about their own and others performance. The judgements may be about the execution of the movement, or about the structure of the dance.
- Use this knowledge to improve the quality and the variety of their performance. This could relate to practising and improving work but may also relate to the structuring of the dance.
- Sustain energetic activity over appropriate periods of time and show that they understand the affect of exercise on the body. The dance lesson may have a particular focus on the preparation for activity, children may undertake the mobilisation of the body, the warm up and cool down by the end of the stage.

To use the statements for assessment of achievement or learning

- identify an appropriate statement from the descriptor
- determine the nature of the statement
    - is it a statement of physical achievement?
    - is it a statement of learning or understanding?
- observe and decide if the child is
    - working towards the statement
    - has achieved
    - is working beyond the description.

The categories of achievement are as suggested by SCAA in 1996, and are simple to use. Looking at the videotape and reading the literature on the exemplification of standards (SCAA1997) will demonstrate assessment using these principles. Assessment in Physical Education is demanding but it is by no means impossible. Teachers who consider that they have no experience in assessment of dance may in fact have more skill than they realise. Use the model of competencies in assessment to identify your abilities and determine your next stage of development

Model of Competencies in Assessment

● Competencies associated with managing observation

I have the ability to:

- scan and observe the room generally, see whether the children are on task
- observe the achievement of individuals, see who is not on task, see who is performing well.
- observe the movement skill or competence of a child in relation to the developmental stage or a movement quality, such as fluency.
- observe a range of children in the same way.
- systematically observe the whole class in this way.

Systematic observation of the class may prove challenging but a number of strategies can be tried.

● Competencies associated with identifying the focus of assessment (what is being assessed)

I have the ability to:

- identify appropriate indicators of skill development or movement vocabulary. For example, what will show that the child can perform a simple skill safely? The child will move with bodily control and without collision with others.
- identify the indication of other learning. For example, what will show an understanding of the space? The child will move using different levels and directions.
- use the EKSDs as assessment criteria.

● Competencies associated with enabling reporting

I have the ability to:

- find strategies for assessment against the EKSDs.
- find strategies for recording my assessment.

Strategies to help teachers manage assessment recording and reporting

● Managing observation

Build observation into your planning.

- try to observe a particular group of children throughout the lesson.

- each lesson ask a different group of children to show their work and make this an observation time
- If you are assessing an aspect of learning not directly related to motor performance, for example, the ability to work with others or to contribute ideas for dance, watch or work with a particular group for a significant time in the lesson.
- video-recording lessons or final presentations may be helpful, but reviewing the material may be time consuming.
- Decide what you are assessing and be clear about the criteria. Many aspects of movement are used in any one PE lesson but if the learning objective is clearly stated in the planning the assessment will normally relate to this. Assessment of learning or understanding may be shown through talking about the activity, this is particularly true of the understanding of the health-related dimension of Physical Education. Understanding can also be shown through performance: if a child uses different levels and directions in a piece of work, that can evidence understanding of the use of space.

Recording the achievements of dance

Recording observations or assessment is important, it creates evidence and allows the teacher to have a statement of achievement or understanding to share with parents or other professionals. It may be possible to reflect and note brief observations after lessons; this anecdotal evidence could be used for children of particular ability or those who are on individual education plans.

For more general assessment, simplicity and brevity are crucial, a realistic record may be on a chart:

PE POS Dance				Date		
Unit Title: Making a dance with partners				KS:		Year:
Movement objective: to create a dance with a clear start & ending						
Assessment criteria: the dance will have a known & constant start & ending						
Other objective: to work with others						
Assessment criteria: can make a dance with a partner						
Name	First objective			Second objective		
William	[towards] √	[achieving]	[beyond]	[towards]	[achieving] √	[beyond]

Table 5.1 *Record of Attainment*

(The tick boxes indicate that William is working towards the first movement objective and has achieved the second objective.)

Children can contribute to the recording of dance achievements. At both key stages they can comment on the dance or their achievements in terms of movement ability or knowledge.

- **KS1** children can draw a favourite dance activity and older children can write a sentence about their dance.
- **Older KS1 & KS 2** children can record the sequence of their dance and may also make a statement of learning or achievement at the end of a unit of work.

The use of a **writing frame** can help children assess and record their learning as well as set targets for future development.

Example:
  At the beginning of this unit, I could ....
  At the beginning of this unit I could not ....
  Now I am better at ....
  Now I can ....
  Next I want to learn to ....

Example:
  When I began I was not good at ....
  I have learnt to ....
  I am better at ....
  I still need to work at ....
  I am most pleased that I ....

A **learning log** may be used throughout a unit of work.

At the start of the unit:
  I can
  I want to be able to.

Each lesson:
  I was good at
  Today I tried hard to
  Today it was hard to
  I can nearly
  Now I can
  Next I want to work at,
  I want to be able to
  I have learnt that.

At the end of the unit:
  I can

I have learnt
Now I understand.

Implementing a simple policy of recording at the end of a unit of a work would impact on the awareness of dance through the school. Children can begin to have a sense of their own development, and the focus on what has been learned will heighten the expectation of learning and achievement in dance. Assessment should not become overwhelming, the use of a portfolio of strategies, including child records, can lead to a broad picture of pupil development.

Dance can contribute to the PE report; as in the following examples.
At Key Stage 1:

> *Peter is able to link the actions of travelling, turning and stopping with control.*

At Key Stage 2:

> *Ruth is able to tell her partner about the sequence of the dance or is able to tell a partner about the pathways and actions of the dance.*

Assessment is integral to effective teaching. Earlier in this chapter you were encouraged to recognise the skills you have. Now decide which assessment strategy you will try to implement in your next sequence of lessons.

Developing dance through the school

Earlier chapters have been concerned with the content and process of dance across the curriculum. This final chapter focuses on issues and strategies associated with the development of dance throughout the primary school. Access to all supporting staff and raising the profile of the subject will enhance the development of dance. The National Curriculum Programme of Study has placed dance firmly on the curriculum but many teachers know that some pupils have attitudes which may need to be challenged or changed.

▶ DANCE FOR ALL

'Boys don't do that' was the comment of one mother on hearing that her son had been involved in a dance lesson. This suggests that if boys sometimes complain when they are told that the PE lesson is dance, they may be reflecting societal attitudes. Just as it is important for children to know the lesson objective, it is also important that we talk to them about the benefits of dance. It should be explained that dance helps you to have a good awareness of your body and this in turn makes you a better games player; that understanding the flow of movement through your body and efficient weight transfer will make you a more skilful mover in the game situation as you dodge and mark. Children should be helped to understand that in dance they learn through experience about space and sensitivity to others, both are important to the member of a games team. Some teachers find that boys enjoy physical challenge within dance – the aerobic warm-up and strong energetic movement. Certainly these should both feature in the curriculum but with care to maintain a balanced programme for all children.

Dance should be available to children who have Special Educational Needs.

Work with children and adults has confirmed the belief that pupils with physical limitations may have a strong kinaesthetic sense and love moving. Inclusion in the lesson will need to be individually negotiated and may involve the classroom assistant alongside the child. Key Stage 2 children may enjoy watching videotape of integrated dance companies such as Canduco. The local Dance Agency or Arts Council will know of any local integrated company whom you may contact. The child who has difficulty with language and other learning skills may also enjoy movement, but it is a false assumption that such pupils will be good at all aspects of dance. It may be that they achieve well in term of performance but are less able in dance-making and evaluation. At times teachers may consider grouping such children with those more able in composing dance. Whatever the performance product of the child it is the experience of moving and dancing alone and with others which is educative.

SUPPORTING STAFF, AUDIT, RESOURCES AND STRATEGIES

A dance audit

Essential to the development of dance in a school is gaining understanding of the particular situations of the school. Audit is a means to this understanding. However informally it is achieved there is a need to know wheat exactly is going on. Key questions may be:

- Is dance taught in each year?
- How much dance is taught?
- Are learning objectives clearly stated?
- Is there any evidence of an expectation of progression?

Policy and planning documents will record what is taught but engaging in conversation with colleagues will give some insight into actual practice. A next step in the way forward may be a questionnaire to staff:

- What is your main difficulty in teaching dance?
- What support or in-service would be most helpful?
- Have you any ideas or resources which you find particularly helpful?

Resources

Resources for dance and music and dance ideas are frequently identified as staff needs.

Chapters 2 and 3 give suggestions for the development of dance ideas, but there is still a place for creating a school resource file. A bank of 'dance cards' may identify the stimulus, music and suggestions for relevant movement teaching. If the process of developing dance cards can be shared with staff this becomes a staff development activity. Staff can be asked to contribute to a collection of pictures or poems to act as stimuli.

Music

Whilst not essential to every lesson, music does enrich the dance experience. Dance can also extend the children's musical experience as different types of music are introduced. Lively rhythmic music for warm-ups may include jazz, dixie or rag. Calm flute sound or music with a with a slower tempo may suit some topics, whilst dramatic works can themselves become a stimulus for the dance. Music of different ethnic styles will also be valuable.

Suggestions:

- Ask each teacher to find a short piece of music for warm up and make a school tape. Similarly ask for any music suitable for dance to be given to the music bank.

- Work with the music teacher to extend the music repertoire and to integrate the dance and music programmes where possible.

- Invite the children to select and collect music for dance. It is a part of the creative process to select music or accompaniment. Many of the dance ideas in this book have suggestions for music with them but any list is particular to the teacher or school, compiling your own collection is important.

- Together with the music co-ordinator, hold a percussion workshop. Allow staff to explore the texture of sound and to experiment with rhythms for movement. The percussion available in the dance space should include, a tambour, tambourine, cymbal and beater, wood blocks or claves and maracas.

Videotape

Looking at other peoples performance can enrich children's dance knowledge and help children to develop critical skills. Viewing dance with children is an experience that will allow the teacher and class focus on a particular aspect of dance making or performance which they are working on. Videotaped dance material is available from the National Resource Centre For Dance and from the Video Place.

Strategies

Strategies to support teachers in planning and delivering the dance

Appendix I
Useful addresses

The Arts Council of England
Dance Department
14 Great Peter Street
London SW1P 3NQ
Tel: 0171-973 6489
National Dance Agencies will help
with regional dance information

Dance 4
Preset
3–9 Hockley
Nottingham NG1 1FH
Tel: 0115-941 0773

Dance City
Peel Lane
Off Waterloo Street
Newcastle Upon Tyne NE1 4DW
Tel: 0191-261 0505

Dance Northwest
Main Office:
PO Box 19
Winsford
Cheshire CW7 2AQ
Tel: 01606-863 845

Dance Xchange
Birmingham Hippodrome
Birmingham B5 4TB
Tel: 0121-622 3253

The Place (National Dance Agency)
17 Duke's Road
London WC1H 9AB
Tel: 017-387 0161

Suffolk Dance
Northgate Arts Centre
Sidegate Lane West
Ipswich IP4 3DF
Tel: 01473-281 866

Swindon Dance
Town Hall Studios
Regent Circus
Swindon
Wiltshire SN1 1QF
Tel: 01793-463 210

Yorkshire Dance
3 St Peter's Buildings
St Peter's Square
Leeds LS9 8AH
Tel: 0113-243 8765

The English Folk Dance & Song Association
Cecil Sharp House
2 Regents Park Road
London NW1 7AY
Tel: 0171-485 2206

The Dolmetsch Historical Dance Society
Hunter's Moon
Orcheston
Salisbury
Wiltshire
Tel: 0980-620339

Contact the local dance agency or the local arts council for information about integrated dance companies and local information of performers and dance practitioners from other cultures.

Dance videotape resources are available from:
The Video Place Tel: 0171-383 0516

National Resource Centre for Dance
University of Surrey
Guilford, Surrey GU5 5XH
Tel: 01483-259 316

The Arts Council or local Dance Agency will provide information on integrated dance companies and groups who promote the dance of specific cultures.

Appendix II
Suggested further reading

● **Publications relating to the National Curriculum**

DFE, 1991, *National Curriculum PE Working Group Interim Report*, HMSO.
NCC, 1992, *Non-Statutory Guidance: Physical Education*, presented with
DFE, 1992, *Orders for Physical Education in the National Curriculum*, HMSO.
DFE, 1995, *Key Stages 1 & 2 of the National Curriculum – Physical Education*, HMSO.
NCC, 1990, Robinson, *The Arts 5 – 16 Practice and Innovation*, Oliver & Boyd.
NCC, 1990, Robinson, *The Arts 5 – 16: A Curriculum Framework*, Oliver & Boyd.
OFSTED, 1998, *The Arts Inspected*, Heineman.
SCAA, 1997, *Expectations in Physical Education at Key Stages 1 & 2*.
SCAA, 1997, *Use of Language Key Stage 1 & 2 – Physical Education*.
QCA, 1998, *Maintaining Breadth and Balance At Key Stage 1 & 2*.
OFSTED 1996–7, *Standards in the Primary Curriculum*.
OFSTED 1996–7, *The Annual Report of Her Majesty's Chief Inspector of Schools*.

● **Books on the nature of dance and the process of dance making**

Autard Smith, 1996, *Dance Composition*, 3rd Ed, Black.
Applebee, 1989, 'The Enterprise we are part of: Learning to Teach' in
P. Murphy and B. Moon (eds) *Developments in Learning and Assessment*, Open University Press, Hodder and Stoughton UK.
Adshead, 1988, *Dance Analysis Theory and Practice*, Dance Books.
Best, 1985, *Feeling and Reason in the Arts*, Allen & Unwin.
Blom & Chaplin, 1989, *The Intimate Act of Choreography*, Dance Books.
Brinson, 1990, *Dance as Education*, Falmer.
Copeland & Cohen, 1983, *What is Dance?* OUP.
Fraleigh, 1987, *Dance and the Lived Body*, University of Pittsburgh Press.

Jordan, 1992, *Striding Out*, Dance Books.

Laban, 1992, *The Mastery of Movement*, 4th Ed., Northcote.

McFee, 1992, *Understanding Dance*, Routledge.

McFee, 1994, *The Concept of Dance Education*, Routledge.

Ross, 1983, *The Claims of Feeling*, Falmer.

Sheets Johnstone, 1979, *Phenomenology of Dance*, Dance Books.

Sheets Johnstone, 1984, *Illuminating Dance*, Lewisburg University Press.

Appendix III
Staff development material

What do you find most difficult about teaching dance?

- Finding ideas for dances
- Finding music for dance
- Knowing what movements to teach/practice
- Knowing how to improve the quality of children's movement
- Helping children to structure dances.

FROM A STIMULUS TO A DANCE

Stage 1 Identifying the relevant movement for the stimulus, theme or topic.

stimulus word	action	space	dynamic quality	relationship

Stage 2 Creating movement action tasks from this knowledge.
Action tasks for the movement teaching will be . . .
Motifs can be developed from the actions of . . .

Stage 3 Forming the dance.
Will the dance be a class dance, a solo, partner or group dance?
Will the class help to decide on the form?
How might we start?
Does the dance have a sequence or story?
How might it end?

POS		Date	Year Group
Resources		Evidence of learning	
		Evidence of learning	
Movement objectives			
Other learning objectives			
Movement Task	Observation points	Grouping	Resources/Safety
Introduction			
Development 1			
Development 2			
Conclusion			
Planning check: where can the children plan, perform and evaluate in this lesson?			

Table A.3: *PE lesson plan (alternative layout)*

PE unit of work	Date	Year	Class
POS	Unit title		
Movement objectives	Evidence of learning		
Other learning objectives	Evidence of learning		
Movement objectives	Observation points	Grouping	Resources
week 1 – – –			
week 2 – – –			
week 3 – – –			
week 4 – – –			
week 5 – – –			
week 6 – – –			
Planning check: what will the children know, understand or be able to do as a result of this unit of work?			

Table A.4: *PE unit of work plan (alternative layout)*

Index